Praise for "Happiness: The Art of Living with Peace, Confidence and Joy"

The clarity and thoughtfulness that Smith brings to this book have been distilled through years of teaching a class on happiness at DePauw University, and he offers clear advice with quiet authenticity, grace and none of the distasteful aggressiveness that can be found in the methods of some self-help books. Smith's tools are simple but not simplified, aiming for, in the words of Oliver Wendell Holmes, "simplicity on the other side of complexity." He neither turns his back on his corporate past nor insists on applying a CEO's toolset to a more mindful approach to life, making his words more broadly appealing. Smith tells his own life story, sharing the challenges and successes he found in articulating and manifesting the skills of happiness, and how he enriched his life by spending time alone in nature and with his wife and two sons. He shares his journey confronting the realities of his illness—chronic lymphocytic leukemia—while trying to nurture five thing in life: "grace, gratitude, courage, peace, and time," each with deep sincerity. Yet he doesn't infuse his own narrative with a much grander meaning, as can be common in books written by those who teach from their own lives. Instead, his well-articulated though not quite groundbreaking story helps by sharing one way to find personal joy by focusing on how we relate to ourselves and others. A big thinker turns his mind to the essence of his happiness in a memoir that's easy to read and maybe even follow.

—Kirkus Reviews

"Read this book with joy and gratefulness as I did and it will lead to happiness."

—Mark Liponis, M.D.
Canyon Ranch Corporate Medical Director Author,
"Ultra-Longevity" and "Hunter/Farmer Diet Solution"

"In confronting life's triumphs, as well as personal challenges, Doug Smith emerges with a balance and view that is remarkable. His book draws you into his personal journey and his insights have application to our everyday lives."

—Richard P. Mayer
Former CEO of Kraft Foods; Former CEO of KFC

"From a ledge on White Pine Mountain, the oracle of happiness identifies the secret sauce of life, and shares it in poignant stories and easy-to-follow teachings. Carve out some quiet alone time, and let Doug share his journey and teachings with you."

—John Lowe
CEO, Jeni's Splendid Ice Creams

"Doug has approached the subject of happiness in the same way he solves business problems: with humor and analytics, intertwined with razor-sharp thinking and writing."

—Parker MacDonell
Principal, Invergarry Partners

"Doug Smith's generously honest book offers wise guidance to readers interested in pursuing a happy life. His infectious optimism and love for the world are reflected throughout this book, and his open and genuine narration of his own journey towards happiness is inspiring."

—Brian Casey
President, DePauw University

"Doug's book should be on everyone's bedside table to remind us, in troubled times, that we can overcome obstacles with mindful attention to finding meaning, purpose, flow and cherishing others. Doug gives generously and honestly of his life's experiences so that we, his readers, will know that we are not alone."

—Nancy Williams
Executive Director, Lake George Land Conservancy

"Reading this book will benefit everyone; for many it will be life-changing; for some it may be life-saving. Heartfelt, moving and impactful, a must read for all."

—H. S. Sunenshine, PhD
Former President, Walker Research

"Take a journey with Doug Smith's 'Happiness'. It is a remarkable book and personal story that I highly recommend. This book will make you smile and maybe even start you on your own journey toward achieving a higher level of personal contentment and self-actualization."

—Peter R. Dolan
Former Chairman and CEO of Bristol-Myers Squibb

"Happiness . . . That warm and fuzzy thing, right?? No. Absolutely not. It's that necessary and very real thing we all seek. Doug shares his life experiences while teaching us the skills of happiness in a very moving and real way."

—Andrew R. Summerfield
President & Creative Director, Summerfield Advertising

"This powerful book guides us along a path of faith and determination to reach our dreams through forgiveness and compassion."

—Prof. em. Dr. Guido Mislin
ETH, Zürich.

"Doug Smith brings great insights to an extremely important topic. It makes terrific reading for anyone going through life changes and challenges."

—Stephen Sadove
Former Chairman and CEO, Saks

"When adversity found him, Doug found happiness, and, in so doing, blazed a path that many readers will benefit from following."

—Josh Sommer
Executive Director, Chordoma Foundation

"With a business leader's smarts, a father's love, a husband's devotion, Doug tackles the questions of happiness in his own life and gives away the secrets to his readers."

—John P. Schuster
Author of "Answering Your Call" and "The Power of Your Past"

"Doug Smith provides us all with a truly rare and unsparingly honest glimpse into the inner life of a CEO—and one man's journey from being driven by fear and judgment, to leading from love and happiness. The concepts and skills Doug describes are invaluable to us all."

—Ken Murphy
Former EVP of Human Resources, Altria

"The lessons in this book are a poignant reminder that the values of gratitude, friendship, forgiveness and optimism are universal and true for all of us. This is a moving story of one blood cancer survivor's journey, his story will inspire other patients and their families who are living with a blood cancer, as well as anyone who wants to pause for a moment and reflect on themselves and their impact on others . . ."

—John E. Walter
President & CEO, The Leukemia & Lymphoma Society

"This book is a gift that has made me a better father, better friend and better leader. This book is the most important book I have read in years."

—Tom Krouse
President, Donatos

"In the true spirit of altruism, encouraged within these pages, Doug has graciously given us the gift of better understanding how to find happiness."

—Dennis Bland
CEO, The Center for Leadership Development

HAPPINESS

The Art of Living with Peace, Confidence and Joy

by
Douglas A. Smith

Published by
White Pine Mountain
445 Hutchinson Ave., Ste 270
Columbus, OH 43235

2nd Edition, 2014.

ISBN: 978-0-9860708-0-8

Library of Congress Control Number: 2013954900

Printed in the United States of America.

To Sparky

and

*To everyone working
to make it a
cancer-free world*

TABLE OF CONTENTS

APPENDIX

My great-grandfather told how during the Great Famine, when everyone around his part of the country was starving, a crow flew past with a potato in its beak, which meant it was a good potato, not diseased, and men, women and children set off after the crow, stumbling into ditches, falling, jostling each other to be the one to get the food if the bird dropped it. That's what the pursuit of happiness is like. This is one of life's mysteries there is no coming to terms with — that as long as we have breath we have no choice but to go running after happiness, our poor faces strained upward as if we cannot get enough of it, as if happy is what we were meant to be, as if without happiness we would starve. As we would.

—Nuala O'Faolain, *Chasing the Evanescent Glow*

PROLOGUE

This is a book about happiness. More specifically, it is about my own journey to discover and increasingly practice the skills that lead to happiness. It is not about plastering a smile on my face or always being in a good mood. It is about something much deeper, much more fundamental.

What I am seeking to know more about, better practice and share with others, is that which enables certain people to have an underlying and predominant sense of well-being and contentment even in their darkest, most difficult days. Genuinely happy people, I believe, have a kind of ballast that lets them meet with the loss of a job, a broken relationship, a major health challenge, a financial reversal or any number of setbacks, and still bounce back. They realize that anger, remorse, guilt and denial are all stages; they aren't permanent places of residence.

I further believe what enables happy people to have this resilience is a set of skills that give them a perspective about three things. The first is that they remember the past with peace. They don't carry around a lot of remorse or anger about the past. They have learned from whatever adversities they faced and mistakes they made, and then they have moved on.

Second, they anticipate the future with confidence. As they look to the future, they plan and prepare for it, but they also realize they cannot control it. They recognize that the future will invariably be different than the scenarios they envision. How they adjust to the diversions the universe invariably takes sets them apart from others who face the future with rigidity.

Finally, with the ability to let go of the past and to be confident about the future, happy people live in the present with joy. It has been suggested that happiness is found in two places, in the present and within us. Genuinely happy people have the skill to both be in the present and to look deeply within themselves and find happiness.

While the skills that enable this perspective are ones we will never perfect, learning to better practice these skills can have a profound effect on our own happiness.

This book is based on four premises:

Everyone wants to be happy. This is true without exception. We all have a deep yearning to live happily. In fact, the goal of achieving happiness underlies every decision we make. Whether we take a job or don't take a job, get married or don't get married, have kids or don't have kids, give money or don't give money — we think whatever we decide will bring us greater happiness. Happiness is what philosophers call an "ungrounded grounder." Meaning that "because it will make me happy" is the ultimate answer in a long list of "whys." Once we reach that point, there is no further grounding needed.

Happiness is hard. It is easy to be unhappy. It is living with joy that is difficult. This is particularly true when we feel at odds with the world and face adversity and setbacks.

Happiness is a skill. Happiness is hard because it is a skill. This might be the most profound thing I have learned on my journey. Previously, I had not thought about happiness as a skill. In fact, it is a set of skills. Like all skills, happiness has a genetic component. But also, like all skills, we can study the skills of happiness and, through practice, become increasingly proficient. We can become happier.

Happiness is worthy of study and pursuit. There is overwhelming research demonstrating the benefits of being happy. Those of us who are happiest have healthier, more enduring and more satisfying relationships. We do better at work, are more productive, are better able to work with others and even earn more money. We have better physical and mental health. We live longer. The benefits of being happy are immense.

This book is organized around my own journey to become more proficient at the skills of happiness, beginning with a life transition some nine years ago. As a result of my journey, I have become better at practicing the skills of happiness. I am happier. My hope is that by sharing my journey, which has really just begun, others will come to better understand and better practice the skills of happiness. My hope is that you, the reader, will be happier.

I also hope you enjoy the journey.

Douglas A. Smith
October 2013
At the foot of White Pine Mountain

MORNING
ON THE OTHER SIDE
OF COMPLEXITY

I wouldn't give a fig for simplicity on this side of complexity, but I would give my life for simplicity on the other side of complexity.

—Oliver Wendell Holmes

Chapter 1

Sunrise from White Pine Mountain

November 2012

If you can meet with Triumph and Disaster,
And treat these two impostors just the same . . .
And lose and start again at your beginning . . .
Yours is the earth and everything that's in it.
        —Rudyard Kipling, select lines from *If*

Lake George sits tucked among the Adirondack Mountains of upstate New York near the border with Vermont. At 32 miles long it is the largest lake in the 6-million-acre Adirondack Park. The park is a patchwork of public and private land that covers about one-fifth of New York State, but contains only a fraction of its population.

In the early 1800s paper and lumber companies clear cut millions of acres in upstate New York, and then moved west to find virgin timber. They left behind land that had been stripped and they viewed as worthless, so when they stopped paying taxes on the land, it reverted to the state. In the late 1800s New York decided such devastation of its land would never happen again. To ensure this, they created the Adirondack Park in 1892, setting much of the state land aside as "forever wild." It's funny how good things often come from such troublesome events.

My father and mother purchased a small piece of lakefront property in 1945, as the Second World War came to an end. My dad, J. Stanford Smith, was an Indiana farm boy who thought Lake George and the mountains that surrounded it were like nothing he had ever seen. In 1936 he began a career at General Electric in Schenectady, New York, about 70 miles south. Electricity was a key to the future in the 1930s, and my father intended to be part of that future — in fact, he intended to lead it single-handedly, if necessary.

In 1938 he married my mother, Elaine Showalter, who also grew up in Indiana. They had met while students at DePauw University. In 1946, they built a small cabin on the west side of the lake, in the village of Hague. They called the humble cabin "Barcastedo." The name was probably intended to sound Native American in origin, but it is actually the first few letters of my siblings' and my names — **Bar**bara, **Ca**rol, **Ste**ve and **Do**ug. The cabin sits in a small bay sheltered by nearly a dozen islands. The land and home have now passed to my siblings and me.

During July and August, Lake George and the Adirondacks are a vacation Mecca for the people of New York and surrounding states. But after Labor Day it belongs to the few year-round residents. Within the park there are only 100,000 permanent residents, about the same number that lived here in 1900. These residents have mixed feelings about the summer folk. I suppose most of them would prefer to have the lake and mountains to themselves all year, but tourism is an essential source of livelihood to the people of the Adirondacks. Hague is no exception. The resorts, boating industries and caretaking the property of summer residents all provide needed work. A pillow at the home of a close friend and neighbor captures perfectly the sentiments of the year-round residents: "God bless everyone . . . even the summer folk."

~

In early November 2012, I am at the lake. I have come alone for 10 days of solitude; to study, to read, to reflect and to write. I clearly have an understanding wife. As I do most every morning when at the lake, I have hiked up White Pine Mountain, which stands behind our house.

I have been sitting on a ledge overlooking the lake since just before sunrise. The sun has now risen well over the mountains on the eastern shore. The sky is the bright blue one only seems to find in autumn. The leaves have just about finished their annual show of color. The shores of the lake are a patchwork of colors — green from the hemlocks, white pine, spruce and fir trees and yellow, red and orange from the oak, maple, hickory and beech trees that share the mountain sides. Being late fall, the tourists have left and the lake is quiet, with only the sounds from an occasional fishing craft interrupting the stillness. I wear a wool sweater and a heavy jacket, as the chill of the approaching Adirondack winter overwhelms the warmth of my fading summer memories.

As I sit looking out over the lake and the sun rises over the mountains, I am filled with an overwhelming sense of awe and gratitude that I have the privilege of being here. By "here" I suppose I mean this particular spot, on this particular day. But in a larger context, I realize that the overriding and predominant feeling in my life is a deep sense of gratefulness for the fortune just to be on this earth in possession of the capacities of a "normal" human being. It seems I thank God dozens of times each day for the privilege of just being alive. I feel as if my life is a miracle beyond comprehension and that my being "here" is an incredible gift. Put simply, the predominant feeling in my life is joy.

I haven't always felt this way. In fact, as I look back over my 66 years, I realize through much of my life I have been a selfish little nerd, complaining, moaning and whining that the world would not bend itself to my particular whims and desires. In many ways I feel as if much of my life has played out with me as a passenger traveling through some of the most incredibly beautiful terrain with my eyes closed.

The sun comes out from behind a cloud and shimmers on the water, and I smile as I contemplate the irony surrounding the events of some eight years earlier that have led me to the other side, to this higher ground. These strange events have opened my eyes and given me this overwhelming sense of gratitude, peace and love for the life I have been given.

COMPLEXITY

Chapter 2

THE LONG RIDE HOME

*In the depth of winter, I finally
learned that within me there lay
an invincible summer.*

—Albert Camus

Have you ever asked a question and then realized you desperately don't want to hear the answer?

It is early September 2004 and I am sitting in a hematologist's office at Mayo Clinic in Rochester, Minnesota. I'm here because of some rather strange blood test results I received a couple of months earlier, followed by even stranger MRI results. My general practitioner in Columbus, Ohio, has suggested I see a hematologist.

I consider myself to be in good health. I have few aches and pains. At 58 my prostate may not be quite the same as it was at 18 and I have had my hips replaced, but this hasn't held me back. When I get up most mornings I walk 3 or 4 miles. I feel fine and as a result I have concluded that these test results are flukes and that the doctors at the Mayo Clinic will confirm my diagnosis.

After two days at the Mayo Clinic of probing and testing me, the doctors seem to be coming to the same conclusion. One more appointment with the hematologist, who has run a series of blood tests, and I will be out of there, heading back home to Columbus with a clean bill of health.

The hematologist has received results from most of the blood tests and they are, as only doctors can say it, "unremarkable"— meaning they are normal. We exchange a few pleasantries and I'm about to walk out the door when, just like in the movies, the phone rings. The doctor picks up the phone, listens for a couple of minutes, hangs up, writes something down and slowly turns toward me. Then he tells me as compassionately as he can that the results of the final test are not good. They reveal that I have a form of blood cancer. Specifically, I have Chronic Lymphocytic Leukemia (CLL), which he tells me is slow developing but incurable. I slowly take in what he says.

So I ask the question I wish I hadn't asked. It is probably the same question most of us would ask, at least to ourselves, if not to the doctor, upon receiving such news: "How long before this illness ends my life?" As soon as the words are out of my mouth, I begin to realize I don't want to know the answer. But before I have the time, the clarity of thought or the courage to retract it, I find myself hearing the answer.

"CLL is a disease that runs from being indolent, never even requiring treatment in one's lifetime, to much more aggressive forms that can be very difficult to manage," he says.

I guess I looked like I wanted to hear more because he then added: "Your pathology report indicates you may have a more aggressive form of the illness, or that you contracted it some time ago. With existing means of treatments, I think you can probably count on living another five to 10 years. It could be less, could possibly be even more. No one can know for sure."

I sit in silence. Slowly, I gather my things and try to gather my thoughts as I leave his office and head to the parking lot to find my car. I am overcome with fear. It is about six in the evening and I am alone in the car — except it feels like I have a companion sitting in the passenger seat next to me: death.

My mind is consumed with the diagnosis and prognosis I have been given. I want to call my wife, but I want to collect my thoughts before I do.

I had planned to stay in Rochester and fly home the next day, but a night alone in a hotel room is not very appealing — in fact, it frightens the hell out of me. Columbus is a 12-hour drive. If I leave now, I will arrive around 7 a.m. on Thursday. I continue to sit in the parking lot trying to make sense out of my present situation. Finally, I put the key in the ignition and begin the long overnight drive back to Columbus and the comfort of home.

Cell phones can be wonderful instruments. During the night I call my dear wife Phyllis at least a dozen times. I am driving and she is not sleeping, so we talk. We are on this journey together as we have been on every other journey for the past 35 years.

Between phone calls I try to make sense out of what I have been told. My first thoughts are pretty primitive: Make this illness go away and make this all a bad dream. I hope repeating the sentiment will make the diagnosis and the illness magically disappear. My mind races over the facts that I have learned, sparse as they are. I can't fully comprehend or accept them. How could this be? I feel fine. I haven't done anything that would lead to this diagnosis. Maybe the doctors have it all wrong. Maybe they are reading someone else's blood test results. I play the whole scene with the hematologist over and over again in my mind, looking for a different outcome. Of course, I can't find one, so my mind races on even faster.

I try the radio. Maybe between the country, classical and new age music and the late-night talk shows, I will find an answer. But to what? I keep coming back to the fact that I have cancer, an incurable form at that. What does incurable mean? He said it was slow developing. What does that mean? Maybe it is incurable to western medicine, but maybe some alternative forms of treatment work to "cure" the illness. Maybe I shouldn't be thinking about a cure as much as something that will manage the illness, extend my life . . . maybe even to a fuller expectancy. For someone who is 58, what is a normal life expectancy anyway? My mind then races back to the beginning of this tortuous cycle . . . make this illness go away. I am running on nervous energy, and I am using lots of it. But it is getting me no place. It is like spinning one's tires in the mud and digging a deeper and deeper hole. The phone is my lifeline. I again call my wife. She lovingly tries to get me to slow the pace of my thinking, to drop my primitive thoughts.

I pull over to the side of the road. It is windy, and as I gaze out the window I can see the broken clouds racing across the sky, weaving in and out of the stars and half moon. The night sky is really quite beautiful. I try to slow my thinking and get centered, taking a few deep breaths. I am filled with fear, with anger, with a sense of loss and uncertainty about the future. And then, sitting by the side of the road and looking into the darkness, I begin to feel calmer. For the moment at least, my mind is no longer cycling. I think that maybe, just maybe, I can figure out a way to deal with this. But the thought is fleeting, and the fear returns. I pull back onto the highway heading for the comfort of home.

The country music station begins playing one of my favorite songs, *Save the Best for Last*, performed by Vanessa Williams. As I listen, I begin to hear words I have never really heard before.

> *Sometimes the snow comes down in June,*
> *Sometimes the sun goes round the moon.*
> *It's not the way I hoped or how I planned,*
> *But somehow it's enough.*

As night begins to turn to day, I think back to an earlier challenge. It has been said that with age comes wisdom, but I have learned from personal experience that doesn't always happen. Sometimes age comes alone. I hope now that is not the case for me or Phyllis.

We have been blessed with two wonderful sons, Gordon and Greg. But in 1971 our oldest son Gordon was born prematurely and, due to oxygen deficiency during his first hours of life, was left mentally handicapped. With time we both came to see Gordon as an incredibly beautiful gift. But for me, it was after years of agonizing and self pity about why my son should be handicapped. Now, 33 years later, as I drive through the night, I am determined I will not move back to "Pity City."

I recall an even earlier time in my life. It is a cold winter evening in Scotia, New York, just across the Mohawk River from Schenectady, in 1951 or 1952. It is snowing outside my bedroom window. I am four or five years old and I am getting ready to go to sleep. I say my prayers with my mother:

Now I lay me down to sleep,
I pray the Lord my soul to keep,
If I should die before I wake,
I pray the Lord my soul to take.

We finish the prayer and I ask my mom, "What does 'die' mean?" This, too, is probably one of those questions you don't want answered. She tells me about death. It doesn't sound good. The neighbor's dog had died a few weeks earlier, and that didn't make them any too happy. I tell her I don't want to die and learn that is not an option. I cry. My mother cannot console me and eventually leaves the room, so I can deal with this new-found realization.

Now, 54 years later, I am dealing with the same question and the same fears. I am also feeling that the intervening years haven't brought me any new answers, insights or better ways to deal with my own mortality.

I have often heard people say, "Everything that happens has a purpose." I am not sure this is exactly true. Sometimes, I think things just happen. Once they do, it is our task, with God's help perhaps, to find the purpose in them. But it is not as if God was thinking, "I need to teach Doug a lesson and give

him this illness, or make Gordon be mentally handicapped."
I am sure God has other ways of encouraging me to become
a better person.

I am not a terribly religious person, but I do have my
little conversations with God. Usually they are prayers of
appreciation. I never thought that asking God for something
would do much good. Besides, when I ask God for something,
I always feel a little awkward about it, as if God were some
kind of servant who should do something for me whenever
I choose to call upon him or her. I began feeling that maybe
this time I should get past the awkwardness and ask for
God's help.

With my wife's gentle prodding, I look deeper inside myself
and begin to look for help in changing those things over
which I have power or choice. Before I arrive home in Ohio, I
decide I will ask God to help me find and nurture five things:
grace, gratitude, courage, peace and time. I am not sure
how I came to these five, particularly since I didn't even know
what "grace" was. With time, the relevance of each would be
revealed.

As I turn into the driveway just before dawn, I have a glimmer
of hope that somehow I can deal with this diagnosis. I am not
sure exactly how, but I feel as if with the loving support of
my wife, my family and my friends, and with God's help, I
can somehow come to peace with it. It has been a long night,
and I will have many more difficult moments in accepting my
diagnosis.

I walk through the front door and my wife greets me, tears in
her eyes and a smile on her face.

I am not alone.

Chapter 3

A BLANK CALENDAR

To be in hell is to drift; to be in heaven is to steer.
—George Bernard Shaw

Have you ever longed for a blank calendar? I don't mean a calendar that is blank for a day or two. I mean a calendar that stretches out for weeks, even months, with no scheduled obligations.

When I awoke the first day after my diagnosis, I was feeling anything but blessed. With time, however, I have come to see how blessed I am.

My father was diagnosed with cancer of the pancreas at 67 and was dead within two months. Two of my close friends were diagnosed with cancer after my diagnosis, and have since passed away. By contrast, my own prognosis of five to 10 years would seem like an eternity. Nonetheless, the first week after my diagnosis cancer, fear and loss filled my thoughts. It was as if death was five inches in front of my face.

My father's death from cancer had been quick but not painless. To the contrary, he suffered immensely. He was not ready to die and fought against it with everything he had. His battle ended Jan. 6, 1983, in a hospital in Boston. At 37,

I also was not ready for my dad's death, nor was I ready to contemplate my own mortality.

My neighbor used to say, "You never want to get to know your doctor by his first name." I employed the same tactic with cancer. I studiously avoided learning about it after my dad's death — until my own diagnosis 21 years later.

I began reading everything I could about blood cancer. As with most forms of cancer, the focus is often more about managing it than curing it. Some forms of blood cancer can actually be cured, meaning they do not return. This can be particularly true with more acute forms, where the cancer is fast growing and therefore can sometimes be isolated by chemotherapy. The key to my cancer was to manage it. Although at the time there were several different treatments available, none had been shown to increase life expectancy.

My particular form of blood cancer is very complicated, with hundreds of ways of manifesting itself. Some people have a very indolent form of CLL, which may never require treatment and will not even shorten life expectancy. On the other end of the spectrum, some people have a more virulent form of CLL, which can drastically shorten life expectancy. I began to go through a series of blood tests, scans and bone marrow biopsies to better determine my prognosis. While I have never again asked how long I have to live, I came to realize that given what treatments were available then, my Mayo doctor's first prognosis was probably pretty accurate.

I also came to appreciate that, by fate, I lived 3 miles from the James Cancer Center, a nationally recognized leader in research and treatment of blood cancer. In fact, Dr. John Byrd of the James Cancer Center is one of the top two or three physician scientists in the world finding new approaches to managing my form of leukemia. People travel from around

the world to come to the James, and I can practically walk there.

With several promising drugs in phase III trials for CLL, the way I see it, my timing is either perfect or I got this illness just a couple of years too early. In either event, I and thousands of others are deeply indebted to the tireless efforts of the research doctors and teams that dedicate themselves to finding solutions to various forms of blood cancer. With their help and guidance, these past nine years for me have been glorious. I have felt well, my treatments have had few side effects and I have managed to keep the disease fairly well under control. Thank you to all who dedicate themselves to fighting cancer and other life threatening illnesses.

Phyllis and I began to consider how we wished to spend the years we were being "offered." We spent long evenings talking about the implications. With the help of Chuck Kegler, a trusted friend and lawyer, we began updating our wills. Activities that I once did alone, such as household finances, we began to share so that she would be more familiar with them.

We also began to think about whether I should continue as chief executive of Best Brands. My work had been richly rewarded — probably well beyond what I deserved — and we tended to save a healthy portion of whatever we made and invested it successfully so retiring was clearly an option.

Although I had never considered retirement, it suddenly looked appealing. It would give me the blank calendar I had always thought so attractive. In the prior 15 years I had been CEO of three separate organizations. With each, I had invested myself fully, working far too many hours and days when I should have led a more integrated and balanced life. My wife and two sons had been very tolerant, accepting my long days and hectic travel schedule with a minimum of complaints. As I reflected on my diagnosis and talked it over with Phyllis, I concluded that it was time to let go of these responsibilities.

Two weeks after returning home from the Mayo Clinic, I traveled to Cleveland to visit with our lead investor, Paul Cascio. We had always had an effective and cordial relationship, one based on trust and openness. I shared my diagnosis with him and told him I wished to resign as CEO. Paul agreed to relieve me of the CEO role and asked if I would stay on as chairman. This may be one of the best pieces of information you get from this book: If anyone ever, ever offers you the job as chairman of any organization, for God's sake take it. From my experience, you do absolutely nothing and yet it still sounds great at a cocktail party!

For the first time in my life I had a blank calendar with virtually no career responsibilities or obligations — not just the next few days or weeks, but the emptiness stretched out to eternity. I thought this blank calendar was a blessing. I quickly realized it was a terrible curse.

At first, it seemed a relief. I slept a little later in the morning, took longer walks, enjoyed time with my dear wife and two sons, played more golf. You get the idea. But by November 2004, I found myself sliding into depression.

Those who know me would probably describe me as energetic, upbeat and decisive. Of course, as with all of us, our weaknesses are usually our strengths carried to excess, and this certainly applies to me. I can be much too focused on action, skipping over the important steps of reflection. I can be overly optimistic and I can be controlling when my decisiveness goes astray. In late November 2004, I was none of these things. I was anxious, so unsure of myself that making even simple decisions was painful. I went from being CEO of a billion-dollar business, to quaking when the checkout person at the grocery store asked me, "Paper or plastic?" Sleep was difficult. I would go to sleep around 11 p.m., but by 1 a.m. I was wide awake in a cold sweat.

There are five classic signs of a major depression: a change in sleeping patterns; a change in eating patterns; an inability to make decisions; thoughts of inadequacy; and — the biggie — thoughts of suicide. If you have two or three of these signs, you could well be suffering depression. I had all but thoughts of suicide. While those thoughts never occurred to me, I was experiencing the classic signs of depression.

By definition, someone who suffers depression has mental illness. Yikes! If you are like me, you have never thought of yourself as suffering from mental illness, even if you suffer from depression. But consider this: 10 percent of U.S. adults experience some form of depression in a given year. Half of these qualify as major, or clinical, depression. Women are twice as likely to suffer depression as men, with one in eight women developing major depression at some point in their lifetimes. Nearly 10 percent of adolescents experience depression. Finally, all of these numbers are rising each year. To put it simply, if you experience depression you have lots of company.

Except for the few incidences when I have had depression, I think I have excellent mental health. The U.S. Surgeon

General describes mental health as the ability to do four basic things: engage in productive activity, have healthy relationships, cope with change and deal with adversity. I think I usually do these four things pretty well.

Most historians agree that Abraham Lincoln suffered from repeated bouts of genetically based depression throughout his adult life. In other words, he suffered from mental illness. At the same time, there is no one I think better exemplifies mental health as defined by the surgeon general. Lincoln's ability to lead this nation through one of its most difficult periods, to form deep and abiding friendships with those in his cabinet — even though several of them had previously referred to him as a "baboon" — and to preserve the union in the face of incredible adversity, all the while suffering from depression, demonstrates a remarkable level of "mental health." All of this suggests that no one should be defined by a singular dimension. By doing so, we stigmatize people to their, and our own, detriment.

A few weeks later, Phyllis noticed a book titled *What Happy People Know* in a bookstore. She brought it home for me to read. As it would happen, the book is by Dan Baker, a counseling psychologist at Canyon Ranch, a renowned health and well-being destination, the very place I had decided to head to seek alternative treatments for my leukemia and to deal with my depression. Fortuitous!

The field of psychology has made tremendous strides over the last 30 years in treating depression. The roots of depression are often physical in that the very chemistry of the brain changes. Specifically, depression is often caused by a decrease in the level of neurotransmitters, especially one known as serotonin, which is found in the gaps between the synapses of our brains. Numerous prescription drugs are designed to restore the chemical imbalances of those suffering from depression.

I am one of those people for whom a particular type of anti-depressant known as SSRI (Selective Serotonin Reuptake Inhibitor) works particularly well. You would probably know these medications by their brand names: Prozac, Lexapro and Paxil.

After spending a week in December 2004 at Canyon Ranch in Lenox, Massachusetts and working with Dr. Mark Liponis, who heads Canyon Ranch's medical department, my depression had begun to lift. With the help of Mark and his colleagues, I had learned about meditation, nutrition, exercise and other techniques to deal with the stresses of life and hopefully avoid future depressions.

They also helped me realize that I am a person who needs something to occupy my time and energy. The blank calendar was not the blessing I had expected. I love to use my talents, however humble, in some meaningful way. Escape was not an answer.

Unbeknownst to me at the time, I was discovering one of the key secrets to happiness. I needed to find a new purpose to which to devote myself. The only challenge was: "*What purpose?*" Canyon Ranch, my dear wife, Dan Baker's book had all given me a clue, but I still couldn't see it — yet.

Chapter 4

27 Students, 20 Letters and a New Purpose

It is a peculiarity of man that he can only live by
looking to the future . . . And this is his salvation in
the most difficult moments of his existence.
   —Viktor Frankl, *Man's Search for Meaning*

After returning home from Canyon Ranch, I began to ponder what to do. Doing nothing was clearly not the answer. A phone call several weeks later set in motion a series of events for which I am deeply grateful.

Gary Lemon, a friend and a professor at DePauw University, called in early 2005 and asked if I would be interested in teaching a course on leadership during the winter term in January 2006. Gary heads up an excellent honors program at DePauw called the McDermond Center for Entrepreneurship, and I had done several presentations for his students in the past. After thinking about it, I realized this could be a new purpose toward which to direct some of my energies. I had always loved teaching and the art and science of leadership had been a fascination and passion of mine for years. I accepted the offer.

During winter term at DePauw, students take only one course. This enables them to delve deeply into one subject. To encourage students to do this in areas outside their "comfort zone," grades during winter term are simply pass or fail. Most classes meet four hours a day, four days a week, for about four weeks. Students and faculty get to know each other very well.

DePauw is located in the small town of Greencastle, Indiana, about 40 miles southwest of Indianapolis. Some of its alumni like to describe the university as "the Harvard of the Midwest." Since I attended DePauw, I would suggest this might be a slight exaggeration. But it is a wonderful school. It has about 2,400 students, most of whom graduated in the top 10 percent of their high school class; a stellar faculty; a student-to-faculty ratio of 11-to-1; and a beautiful campus, including a 500-acre nature preserve. I think it is one of the finest undergraduate institutions in the country.

I became a student at DePauw in the fall of 1964, after graduating from Greenwich High School in Greenwich, Connecticut. I wasn't quite in the top 10 percent of my class, but I was number 37 in my extended family to attend DePauw. In May 1908, my grandparents graduated from DePauw and began a long family tradition of attending — and sometimes even graduating. My father graduated in 1936. He often claimed he graduated with the highest academic performance of any student who had ever attended DePauw — his record was safe with me. My mother graduated the same year with honors from the Music School of DePauw. My two sisters attended DePauw in the late 1950s. One cousin graduated with me in 1968 and another cousin graduated a year later. And on the first day of classes my junior year, as I walked into French class, I saw a beautiful woman sitting in the front row. Even though I didn't normally do front rows, I decided to sit next to her. I thought maybe she could be my friend. She could be, would be, has been, is and will always be my best friend, my wife of 44 years. Clearly DePauw is somewhat of a family tradition.

By midsummer 2005, I had made significant progress preparing to teach a course I called "Abundant Leadership." But I had also completed the book Phyllis had given me, Dan Baker's *What Happy People Know*. As the summer progressed, I found I was forming a new interest: understanding what leads to joyful, fulfilling, meaningful, flourishing living. My interest in leadership hadn't really waned; it was just being eclipsed by something about which I began to feel I had to find answers.

At the end of the summer, I called my friend Gary and suggested that I wanted to teach something besides leadership. Gary asked, "What would you like to teach?" "Happiness," I said. Silence. A little more silence. And then, "Tell you what, Doug, why don't you put a syllabus together and let us take a look at it?"

What Gary was really saying was, "Go away!" I didn't. Six weeks later I submitted a syllabus. DePauw accepted the syllabus, probably with a lot of hesitation, but they were kind — and maybe a little curious. On Jan. 4, 2006, I found myself standing before 27 students teaching a winter term course entitled "The Skills of Happiness."

As it turned out, I was not alone in my interest in the topic of happiness. There has been somewhat of a revolution in the field of psychology. I think you can pinpoint the start of this revolution to 1998 when Martin Seligman became head of the American Psychological Association. Each new head of the association picks a theme for the coming year. Martin Seligman chose happiness or, as he termed it, "positive psychology."

Martin Seligman's thinking was pretty simple, but also profound. He thought the field of psychology was "half baked," in that it focused only on illness and not on what led to flourishing, joyful living. The field of psychology had focused on pathology, or mental illness, for all of its 150 years, seeking to cure or manage depression, obsession, bi-polar disorder, schizophrenia, anxiety disorder and other forms of illness. This effort had not been in vain. Through therapy, medication, or the combination of both, many who suffer from these illnesses lead fuller, more productive, happier lives. At some point in our lives, about 25 percent of us will suffer from one or more of these illnesses. Having suffered depression, I can attest that the progress made by the field of psychology is a godsend for many people.

However, the alternative to illness is not necessarily wellness. The question that Martin Seligman wanted psychologists to deal with, in addition to pathological issues, was what leads to flourishing, meaningful, joyous living, or that which enables us to thrive and be happy. Since 1998 the field of psychology has increasingly embraced this question, while continuing to make progress in pathological issues of psychology. In the last 15 years, the same research techniques used to study mental illness have been used to study what leads to happiness. It is as if a new frontier of psychology has emerged and the results are fascinating.

By coincidence, Harvard ("the DePauw of the East"), for the first time in January 2006, also offered a course in positive psychology, or as the students called it, "Happiness 101." The national news channels all picked up on this, with most stories suggesting it was frivolous to offer such a course at an institution for which students, or their parents, were spending $50,000 a year. It seems students didn't feel the same. Eight-hundred-and-eighty-five students signed up for the first Harvard course on happiness, more than had ever signed up for a course before.

In preparing for the DePauw class, I read a couple dozen books on the subject of happiness. Additionally, I became so fascinated that I spent hundreds of hours immersed in every facet of happiness and preparing the lectures. No professor, or "real professor" — since my youngest son Greg likes to say, "Dad, you know you're not a real professor" — could possibly spend that much time on one course.

By the time the first class rolled around, I had built a syllabus that covered the definition of happiness, its historical roots going all the way back to Aristotle, how the mind creates mood, and a look at who is happy and who isn't. The syllabus also covered the role of genetics, circumstances and voluntary choices in happiness; whether happiness is worthy of pursuit; why it is often so difficult for people to achieve happiness; the role of self-esteem in happiness; a set of skills that lead to happiness; and five dead ends to avoid in the pursuit of happiness. The course was a very thorough look at the subject.

The course combined lecture and dialogue. We also devoted a day to Habitat for Humanity in Indianapolis, since one of the keys to happiness is altruism. Required reading included Dan Baker's *What Happy People Know*, Viktor Frankl's *Man's Search for Meaning* and numerous articles by various experts in positive psychology.

After I wrapped up the class the last day of the winter term, the 27 students filed out. Twenty left me handwritten personal letters, some running three pages, expressing their gratitude for the course. In addition, about 10 of my students made an appointment to see the college's president and suggest to him that every student at DePauw should take the course.

Later that night after driving home to Columbus, as I sat in bed, I read each letter and then passed it over to my wife. The letters brought tears to our eyes and we were both humbled with gratefulness, realizing the impact the course has had on the students. The course has had an equally profound impact on me. Phyllis leaned over, smiled and said, "You know you have to teach this again." I said, "No, this was a one-time deal." As usual, within a month or two I came to see things her way and planned to continue teaching.

Six months after first teaching at DePauw, I began teaching at Canyon Ranch, an upscale health and well-being spa. Canyon Ranch is devoted to empowering people to live healthier, longer, more joyful lives. It is probably the granddaddy and the most famous of health spas, founded by Mel Zuckerman and Jerry Cohen in the early 1970s.

At Canyon Ranch my audience was not 18 to 22-year-old college students, but couples, most age 40 and over. I used the same concepts, the same stories and the same materials I used at DePauw. In fact, I changed almost nothing. Yet the response to the Canyon Ranch session was the same as at DePauw — overwhelmingly positive. One woman wrote across the evaluation form: "I have been coming to the Ranch for 20 years and this is the most powerful session I have been to." She then wrote diagonally across the entire page in huge letters: ***"WONDERFUL!!!!!"***

As I began the trip home from Canyon Ranch's facility in Tucson, Arizona, I was feeling pretty smug. I even upgraded to first class, thinking I deserved it. If I were a peacock my feathers would be all fluffed up. We all like approval, but for me, approval is my drug of choice. I seek it far more than I should. I seek approval and when I get it, I am "happy" and when I don't get it, I am "unhappy." Approval strokes my ego, and for most of my life ego was my primary motivator. My journey to find something deeper as a source of motivation, something that inspires versus drives my behavior, is still in the future.

I got to my seat on the airplane. I spread out, since no one was sitting next to me — they could probably see the feathers. I sat back to revel in the approval of the participants in the Canyon Ranch program. I was smiling, feeling good, feeling happy and that was when I heard it — the voice — soft at first, then a little louder.

The voice: "Feeling pretty good aren't you, Doug?"

Me: "Yup, they really loved the program."

The voice: "I guess you really fooled them."

Me: "Huh?"

The voice: "I guess you really fooled them."

Me: "What do you mean fooled them? They loved it."

The voice: "Well, they liked it OK and maybe they will find the ideas helpful, but how about you? Do you find the ideas helpful?"

Me: "Huh?"

The voice: "Well, how helpful are these ideas to you? You gave them 13 skills with which to find peace about the past, confidence in the future and joy and exuberance in the present. How well do you practice these 13 skills and, as a result, do you have peace about the past, confidence in the future and joy in the present?"

Me: "Huh?"

The voice: "Well, are you practicing any of these skills?"

Me: "Hey, that hurts."

The voice: "Well are you?"

Me: "I know a lot about these skills. I have been studying this for months."

The voice: "I didn't ask if you knew about the skills. I asked if you were practicing them."

Me: "Leave me alone."

I asked the steward for a glass of wine. Maybe that would make the voice go away. It didn't.

Me: Silence.

The voice: "Well, let me answer the question for you . . . **NO!** You don't practice most of the skills very well and you don't practice any of them consistently. And as a result, you carry around all kinds of negative stuff from your past, you worry about the future and, to tell you the truth, you are hardly ever in the present as you are distracted by the past and the future and by the myriad things you are trying to focus on all at once."

Me: "I'm not that bad."

The voice: "Why don't you run through the 13 skills and see for yourself how well you practice them?"

Me: "I don't have time."

The voice: "You have time to bask in approval and have folks stroke your ego, but not to evaluate how well you actually practice the skills?"

Me: "Why don't you bug off?"

The voice: "The folks at Canyon Ranch and the students at DePauw don't know you as well as I do. They think you actually practice the stuff you talk about. They think you 'practice what you preach.' You have heard that expression, right? You do know what that means?"

Me: "Who are you anyway?"

The voice: "Your conscience, but you already knew that."

Me: "Go away!!!!"

Of course, it didn't go away, for as H.L. Mencken said, "Conscience is a mother-in-law whose visit never ends."

The voice: "You can fool the folks at Canyon Ranch and your students at DePauw all you want, just don't fool me."

Me: "Damn!"

By now my feathers had all flattened. I was feeling anything but joyous. I pulled out a piece of paper and started rating myself on all 13 skills. I got through four or five of them and abandoned the project. I didn't like what I was discovering. I also realized this was a pattern in my life. I grasp things intellectually, but fail to translate that knowledge to heart and hands. I fail to internalize at a deeper level the things my mind grasps. I fail to move from knowledge to wisdom. Simply put, I often don't practice what I preach.

By the time I landed in Dallas to change planes for Columbus, my peacock moments were long gone. I felt like a hypocrite. I found my gate for Columbus and made my way onto the plane. No feathers, just a tail tucked between my legs this time. The flight from Dallas to Columbus was close to three hours. By the time I arrived in Columbus, I had written down three objectives:

1. Understand what it really means to live happily,
2. Increasingly live my life consistent with that understanding (practice what I preach), and
3. Share that knowledge with as many people as possible.

I also had drawn a big circle around the second objective because it is the step I so often skip. I realized, without achieving the second goal, the third is hollow. As I departed the plane, I realized I had a new set of objectives in my life.

My purpose was found!

THE JOURNEY

Chapter 5

WHAT IT MEANS TO
BE HAPPY

*Where I live in the west of Ireland, often in the
evening a bar of golden light blazes along the horizon
of the ocean. Then small clouds, ragged and wistful,
drift across the radiance and obscure it and thicken,
and that's how the dusk comes. There's nothing I
can do to make the gold arrive, and on its nature it
dissolves. After dusk departs, the dark is not just
dark. It contains the memory of what it was. And
that's what I think happiness is like — radiant like
the last of the sun, but always in the process of
disappearing.*
—Nuala O'Faolain, *Chasing the Evanescent Glow*

It would be helpful if we all could come to a similar conclusion
about what it means to be happy. To do this, I will use
this chapter to share with you some historical perspective
on happiness, as well as insights generated by much of
the recent research conducted in the field of positive
psychology. While we all want to be happy, not all of us have
the same understanding of what happiness is.

Whenever I speak on happiness, one of the first things I seek to address is the common perception that the subject of happiness is somehow unworthy of consideration or discussion. This is particularly interesting when you consider that if you ask parents what they want for their kids, the most prevalent answer by far is: "I just want them to be happy."

In spite of this, in our society we seem to equate happiness with mood, with pleasure, with something ephemeral, with something fleeting, perhaps even frivolous. This has not always been the case. Aristotle said over 2,000 years ago, "Happiness is the meaning and the purpose of life, the whole aim and end of human existence." The Greek word Aristotle actually used was "eudemonia" which means literally "God's spirit within." What Aristotle was referring to was living a flourishing life, which we in turn translated to "happiness."

The founders of our country were not talking about mood or pleasure or anything fleeting when they put the "pursuit of happiness" right up there with "life" and "liberty" in the opening of the Declaration of Independence:

> "We hold these truths to be self-evident, that all men are created equal, that they are endowed by their Creator with certain unalienable Rights, that among these are Life, Liberty and the pursuit of **Happiness** . . . and to institute new Government, laying its foundation on such principles and organizing its powers in such form, as to them shall seem most likely to affect their Safety and **Happiness.**"

The Dalai Lama saw happiness as something worthy of pursuit when he said, "I believe that the very purpose of our life is to seek happiness." He also clearly saw happiness as a skill when he said, "I believe happiness can be achieved through training the mind."

Our country's founders, Aristotle and the Dalai Lama were all talking about something different than mood or pleasure when they talked about happiness. Try substituting "pleasure" for "happiness" in the Declaration of Independence. It doesn't work. Pleasure is something that by definition is fleeting since it depends on a change in outside stimulus. Mood is something that fluctuates day to day, moment to moment.

I believe happiness is more fundamental, more foundational. We are not talking about the giddiness of kids on a playground, or the buzz you get after a couple of beers, or after making your last shopping trip to the mall. In other words, we are talking about something deeper and more meaningful than pleasure. Pleasure is a part of happiness, but it is certainly not synonymous with it. As we will discover later, trying to find happiness primarily through pleasure is a fool's errand.

So what are we talking about? I believe we are talking about an underlying and predominant sense of well-being and contentment. Happiness is an attitude, a way of looking at the world, a perspective. It is not circumstances or pleasure, it is not mood, it is not fleeting or ephemeral, it is not frivolous, or unworthy. Rather, it is at the core of our existence. People who are happy can return to this core again and again, even in times of turmoil and adversity.

Whether we realize it or not, every action we take is for our own happiness. We make decisions on the underlying premise that our choice will make us happier. Philosophers call happiness an "ungrounded grounder." What they mean is that it underlies everything else and requires no further grounding. If you ask someone to explain why they did something, at the end of a long string of "whys" lies the answer: "Because it will make me happy."

The challenge is that often we are not very good at understanding or predicting what will make us happy. We sometimes fail to understand that actions we take in the short term do not lead to happiness or to an underlying sense of well-being and contentment.

Here is how I would capture the essence of what it means to be happy:

> *Happy people have an underlying predominant sense of well-being and contentment. They remember the past with peace, anticipate the future with confidence, and experience and live in the present with joy and exuberance. This attitude is sourced from a life integrated by meaningful purpose and sound principles and enhanced by healthy relationships and appropriate pleasure.*

The happiest among us experience moods, setbacks and adversity, and they feel sorrow and grief just like the rest of us. But they know that sorrow and grief are stages in dealing with setbacks, not permanent conditions or places to reside. At their core, happy people have an underlying and almost always available source of contentment. We have all known people who are constantly in a storm, others who start the storm. Genuinely happy people are often the eye of the storm, where it is calm. They have a foundation that gives them ballast, stability, peace.

When I was a kid I had a Mickey Mouse punching bag. I could punch it, pounce on it, I could even throw it out a second-floor window, and it still popped back up. I think happy people have similar ballast that brings them back to a sense of well-being. They experience financial setbacks and bounce back, illness and bounce back, job loss and bounce back. Perhaps they don't rebound as fast as my punching bag, but they consistently come back to an underlying and predominant sense of well-being and contentment.

To have this sense of well-being, happy people have a set of skills that enable them to learn from the past, but also a sense of peace and serenity about the past. They have somehow released the anger or remorse that keeps us forever in the past. They also think about the future with confidence. No matter what the world throws at them, they believe that somehow they will be able to deal with it. They do not have fear and trepidation about the future. If they can release the past and have confidence in the future, then they can live in the present with joy and exuberance.

With the introduction of positive psychology in the last 15 years, there have been hundreds of studies to determine, among other issues, whether being happy has benefits beyond just feeling good. We no longer have to guess as to the answer. The resounding and consistent conclusion of these research studies is "YES!"

Research shows happy people do better in their careers; have better, more enduring relationships; are more likely to help others and less likely to harm or trespass on others; and have better health. In fact, those among us that are the most happy actually live longer. These research studies are beyond the focus of this book, but they are conclusive: being happy is worthy of pursuit. (If the research is of interest, you can look up the Nun Study and the Mills Longitudinal Study, based on Mills College yearbook pictures, on the Internet. Both are prominent studies documenting the benefits of happiness.)

Thomas Jefferson had it right when he wrote the Declaration of Independence: "Happiness" is right up there with "life" and "liberty."

If you are still somewhat skeptical that happiness is worthy of pursuit, put all the research aside. Think about whether you would rather have a person who is happy or unhappy as a friend, brother, sister, parent, son, daughter, teacher or student? Who would you rather wake up beside every morning? Who would you rather *be*? Happiness is worthy of pursuit.

Another issue I often face when speaking about happiness is the perception that happiness is something we are either born with or not, that we can do little about our level of happiness. As with many misconceptions, there is some truth to this, but only some.

Positive psychologists have determined that there are three factors that determine how happy an individual is, captured in the following equation:

$$H = S + C + V$$

HAPPINESS = Set Point + Circumstances + Voluntary Choices

Modified from Martin Seligman, *Authentic Happiness*

I will walk you through these three factors, describing them and sharing with you their role and importance in our happiness.

Set Point: Set point is our genetic predisposition. It is sourced from our biological parents, not who raised us. The best predictor of our happiness is our parents' happiness. So pick good parents! In this case your parents really did do it to you. In other words, there is nothing we can do about this part of how happy we are.

Circumstances: These are the events and circumstances that affect our lives. Circumstances are what happen to us, both good and bad. While circumstances are somewhat beyond our control, the choices we make in life also shape our circumstances. Circumstances that correlate positively with happiness are marriage, friendships, religion or spirituality, and living in an economically viable "free" country. Circumstances that generally do not correlate in a meaningful way with happiness are leisure, perfect health, race, gender, age (although as we age we become slightly happier), physical attractiveness, and having or not having kids. Income, or money, and happiness have a more complex relationship that is not easily explained by whether or not they correlate with one another — more on this later.

Voluntary Choices: Now here is where things get interesting. Voluntary choices are how we choose to live our lives, how we choose to perceive and respond to the circumstances of our lives. It is the attitude we choose to take or the perceptions we choose to carry. It is how we choose both to think and behave in reaction to whatever circumstance we find ourselves. Our voluntary choices affect our circumstances. Seneca wisely said, "Luck is when opportunity meets preparation." Our circumstances are affected by our ability to learn from mistakes and make better choices in the future. But circumstances are also affected by events well beyond our control. Totally within our control, however, is how we choose to perceive our past, how we choose to anticipate the future and how we choose to live in the present. These are the "voluntary choices."

Since it is the voluntary choices over which we have control, the remainder of this book is dedicated to help each of us shape and enhance these choices in the direction of greater happiness and well-being.

So how much of our happiness is within our control? How much is the result of choices that we make versus genetics and circumstances? Sonja Lyubomirsky and her colleagues at the University of California, Riverside, have studied thousands of people to understand the importance of these three factors in determining our happiness. In general, what they have found is that our happiness is accounted for in the following proportions:

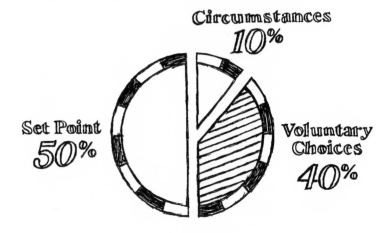

Source: Sonja Lyubomirsky, *The How of Happiness*

What many people find most surprising about this chart is that circumstances account for only 10 percent of our happiness, according to Lyubomirsky's research. Most of us think that circumstances are the primary factor in how happy we are. Circumstances can have a significant effect on our level of happiness, but the vast majority of circumstances, or events, only have such power for a very short period of time.

There are numerous studies looking at people that won the lottery and their happiness levels. After six to 12 months, most lottery winners are about as happy or unhappy as they were before winning. Likewise, those who suffer crippling accidents return near to their previous levels of happiness in a similar time frame. What determines our happiness is more choice than circumstances, more skill than luck.

While some people are naturally better at the skill of happiness, we all can nonetheless develop and enhance this skill. According to the Dalai Lama, we can increase our happiness by "training the mind." So how do we train the mind for happiness? What decisions can we make about how we remember our past, anticipate the future, and live and experience the present that will lead to happiness?

Ah, now those are compelling questions, and ones for which I think I have found some answers. Unfortunately, my journey to these answers has been long and twisted, with numerous dead ends along the way. Maybe by telling my stories, your journey will be less arduous . . . maybe. I hope so.

Chapter 6

Making Peace with the Past

The past is never dead. It's not even past.
—William Faulkner

A few days after returning from teaching Canyon Ranch in Tucson, I decided to make up a chart with the 13 skills I was so adept at teaching, but didn't practice very well. It was probably my mother-in-law conscience that drove me to do this, but however it happened, I created a chart with the 13 skills and had it prominently displayed on both my desk and bathroom mirror (see next page).

As I looked over my chart, I decided I would use it the next time I taught at DePauw or Canyon Ranch, and then that little voice came back and reminded me that first and foremost it was for my use. I always like thinking about how someone else can improve more than thinking about improving me.

Skills That Lead to Happiness

Past	Present	Future
1. Forgiveness	7. Doing now what I'm doing now	3. Faith
2. Gratitude	8. Honoring mind/ body/spirit	4. Optimism
	9. Being Altruistic	5. Flexibility
	10. Thinking with abundance	6. Openness ("FOFO")
	11. Mastering our stories	
	12. Finding meaning/ purpose/flow	
	13. Cherishing relationships	

Thirteen skills were too many to try to practice at once, so I decided to narrow my focus. I decided to start with the past. As I reflected on it, I realized I carried a lot of baggage from the past.

Forgiveness

Just a few days earlier I found myself agonizing about something I had said that was hurtful to my friend John. As I started to recall the situation and then anguish about how

I could have been so inconsiderate, I had to remind myself that John and I were in eighth grade when the exchange occurred. I reasoned that I didn't need to still feel badly about this more than 50 years later. But for some reason, I still did. I often think every stupid thing I have ever done or said is stored away in my mind, ready to be recalled at the most inopportune times. Maybe learning a few new skills about dealing effectively with the past would help.

I started thinking about when I had handled the past well, when I had released something I felt badly about. I realized I had done so when Phyllis and I were first married.

Phyllis and I were married on June 14, 1969, in Baltimore, Maryland. After a short honeymoon in Bermuda, we returned to Baltimore and piled all of our worldly belongings into the back of a Pontiac. We began the long drive to Minneapolis, where I had taken a summer job at General Mills as an assistant product manager on Bisquick Baking Mix. Our route took us across the New York State Thruway past Buffalo and very near Niagara Falls.

When Phyllis travels she likes to stop and see a little bit of the world around her. She isn't driven by some arbitrary arrival time. She also had always wanted to see Niagara Falls and had expressed that to me as we drove along. I, on the other hand, like to drive straight through to wherever we are going.

Somewhere just east of Buffalo, Phyllis fell asleep. I kept driving. As we approached Erie, Pennsylvania, she awoke and asked me where we were. When I told her, she quickly calculated that Erie was west of Niagara Falls. I sheepishly suggested I didn't want to wake her.

I will save you the ensuing conversation by telling you that as we approached Cleveland, Ohio, we turned around and drove the four hours back to Niagara Falls. It was probably late afternoon when we arrived on the American side of Niagara Falls. The parking lot was completely empty. We parked the car and walked over to the observation deck. When we got there we found the falls were gone!

Most readers won't remember this, but in the summer of 1969 the water for the American Falls was diverted to the Canadian side through an elaborate set of levees. This is true. It was done so that engineers could work to remove the boulders at the bottom of the falls that made the American Falls less impressive than the Canadian Falls. Unfortunately, it was later found that they could not remove the boulders without endangering the rock formation under the falls. Soon after, the water was once again allowed to run to the American side without any changes being made, but that was well after our visit.

As we looked at the very unimpressive mud hole, Phyllis made a logical suggestion that we head over to the Canadian side. By now I was ready to move on and forcefully told her so.

We were soon sitting silently in the car driving west toward Minneapolis having never seen Niagara Falls. It was our first major fight as a married couple.

That trip past Niagara Falls was more than 40 years ago, and if you mention the words "Niagara Falls" to my wife . . . she smiles. It would be easy for Phyllis to continue to be angry over what a jerk I was on that trip (and I was a jerk), and it would be easy for me to carry remorse about it as well. In fact, every time anyone mentions anything about Niagara Falls, we both could get upset.

Believe me, it is easy to carry remorse or anger for years, even a lifetime, over considerably more trivial events. William Faulkner's words ring true for many of us: "The past is never dead. It's not even past." But in this particular case, within a few weeks we could both laugh about my thoughtlessness at Niagara Falls and even share the story with friends. My dear wife had chosen to forgive me and I had chosen to forgive myself. We would eventually live in Canada a mere 45 minutes from Niagara Falls, and we visited it many times during our six years of living there. There is justice.

As much as I wish we had, I don't think either of us realized then that we were practicing one of the most important skills of happiness regarding the past: forgiveness. If we had known it, we might have practiced it on so many other issues we faced, often considerably more trivial, where we were less willing to let go and forgive. Time does not heal all wounds; for that you need forgiveness.

Unlike the present, the past does not exist. It is an idea, a thought, a concept, a memory we choose to carry with us. Our only access to the past is our thinking. Being able to remember the past is a wonderful gift. It enables us to learn, to realize consequences of certain behaviors, positive and negative, and therefore change our actions in the future. We can use our memories to relive pleasant or meaningful moments. Memory is wonderful.

Memory can also be a curse. It can keep us up at 3:00 a.m. with regret or anger as we think back on negative past events that we should have released years ago. How we choose to use the gift of memory is a key to happiness.

There are only four actions we can take with negative events in the past. First, we can forget them. This is great, if it happens. But many of the negative things that happen are difficult to forget, and telling ourselves to forget is not a viable strategy. Phyllis and I are never going to forget about the Niagara Falls incident; it is just part of who we are.

Telling ourselves to forget usually results in the second action we can take with negative events; repress them. Repressing events leads to dysfunction somewhere else, since events that are repressed always seem to find their way out in destructive ways.

The third thing we can do with negative events is hold on to them. This is the strategy we probably employ the most. If the event is about something we have done that we regret, we hang on to it to remind ourselves how imperfect we are, often long after we have made amends. If it is about someone else who has hurt us, we keep it as a bargaining chip or as a way of having power over them in the future. Or we keep it with us to gain sympathy from others or to give us a feeling of self-righteousness. We always get something in return for holding on to these hurts, but what we get is a lousy substitute for happiness.

The fourth action we can take with hurts from the past is to forgive. Forgiveness is the only voluntary choice we can make to release negative events in our past, whether they are things we regret doing or things others did to us. Forgiveness is the choice that leads to happiness.

In regards to Niagara Falls, Phyllis and I were both practicing forgiveness, but we were practicing two very different skills. I was practicing forgiveness of self and she was practicing forgiveness of others. Each skill requires its own distinct capabilities. We can be good at one and not the other, good at both, or lousy at each. (I know the last from personal experience.)

Forgiveness of self is about the struggle for self-esteem, about being worthy of forgiveness and therefore worthy of being happy. Nathaniel Branden, one of the country's leading academics concerning self-esteem, defines self-esteem as feeling worthy of happiness and confident that we can face the future. Being worthy and being confident are two keys to happiness. Forgiveness of self is therefore essential to happiness.

Forgiveness of others is different. It is about the ability to release the need or the desire for vengeance, retribution, or to hurt someone who has hurt us, or that we imagine has hurt us. It is about finding within ourselves the ability to release anger.

I think forgiveness is a skill with which most of us struggle — a lot. During one of my winter term classes at DePauw, we devoted a day to forgiveness. I gave a brief lecture on the subject, and then the 33 students broke into groups of five or six to discuss forgiveness at their tables. I was watching from the front of the room, when within 15 minutes there were students crying at every table — and this was a class in happiness!

When I brought the students back together to talk as a group, I asked why they were so emotional about the topic. One student raised her hand and said, "I realized as we talked about forgiveness that I had never fully forgiven anybody for anything. When I mentioned this to the others, they seemed to feel the same way. Forgiveness is a key to happiness, I am only now learning how to exercise."

I don't think she and her classmates are unique. Forgiveness — releasing the desire for vengeance or the feeling of remorse and not having it come back — is one of the most important and difficult skills of happiness. We often say we have forgiven someone or ourselves, but when the event resurfaces, we find we still wrestle deep inside with it. So how do we practice this skill?

First, it helps to recognize forgiveness is a skill. It is not something that just happens, it is something we must consciously decide to practice.

Second, it helps to recognize who is the beneficiary of the gift of forgiveness. Whether we forgive ourselves or someone else, it is a gift we give ourselves. When we forgive someone else we seem to think we are giving them a gift. It often doesn't make a difference to the other person whether we forgive them or not, but it always makes a difference to us . . . a positive difference.

Third, forgiveness is not dependent on someone being worthy of forgiveness. Forgiveness has little to do with justice. Since the forgiver benefits most from forgiveness, holding it back because the recipient may not act in a way that deserves forgiveness, punishes the forgiver, not the person being forgiven.

Thinking back on all of this, I decided I would start practicing a fairly simple — but hard to apply — rule. If I do something that I feel badly about, or if someone does something to me that I am angry about, I am going to start giving myself

48 hours to deal with it. To make amends, say I am sorry, seek out the person who has hurt me and explain why it has hurt me — whatever it is, it has to be done within 48 hours of the event. After that, it is over. I will let it go. Phyllis practices this 48-hour rule, too. We have come to calling it "dumping the garbage."

Let me explain. Think about all the hurts you cause someone and all the hurts someone causes you as pieces of garbage. What we have a tendency to do is collect these events and put them in a garbage sack. Then, most of us carry that sack of garbage around with us for days, weeks, years, even lifetimes. Believe me, it starts to stink. And yet we still don't let it go. We hang on to it to use at some later point. Phyllis and I found that we would be arguing about something and one of us would bring back some hurt from months or even years ago. What Phyllis and I try to do with our 48-hour rule is resolve any hurts we have caused or experienced, and get it out of our life and not bring it back at some later date. Now I know that some hurts take a lot longer than 48 hours to resolve, but many times the things we held on to for years could have been resolved in less than 10 minutes.

Earlier I wrote that my wife smiles when someone mentions Niagara Falls more than 40 years after our row, but many of you likely would not have been surprised if I indicated that she gets red in the face or angry. I can only imagine the toll carrying such anger or remorse around with us for 40 years would take on our health, our kids, our marriage, our friendship, our well-being — our happiness.

Forgiveness is the first key to finding peace, serenity, satisfaction and pride with our past. It is a major step on the pathway to happiness. It is also a skill that takes a lifetime to fully understand and practice, as I have discovered. I also have begun to understand why it works to bring us happiness. It is really pretty simple. It works because forgiveness enables us to get negative things out of our life. Forgiveness enables us to release something for which we are remorseful or something about which we have anger. In other words, it lets us eliminate negative feelings about the past and in so doing it enables us to find greater happiness. Forgiveness is like Tide laundry detergent — "It gets the dirt out!" (If you struggle with forgiveness, Everett Worthington, chair of psychology at Virginia Commonwealth University, is one of the foremost authorities on forgiveness and has written several books on the subject, that may be of help.)

With my 48-hour rule in hand, a better understanding of why forgiveness is so important to happiness and a commitment to better practice forgiveness of self and others, I moved down the list of skills to the second one that deals with the past: gratitude.

Gratitude

Gratitude is many things. It is a sense of wonder about the world. It is appreciating something or someone. It is being thankful for who we are and what we have. It is, as my grandma told me, counting our blessings. It is also a wonderful way to increase our happiness. It is nearly impossible to feel both grateful and unhappy. Gratefulness leads to happiness.

A few weeks after starting to focus on the skill of gratitude, I was at the hospital. To treat my illness and slow its progress, I occasionally must have infusions. The infusions last most of a day and while not necessarily pleasant, they are relatively painless. One infusion happened to fall on my birthday.

It was a beautiful Saturday morning in May — one that I would have much rather spent outdoors playing golf. I was in a bad mood as soon as I woke up and thought about the day ahead, and as soon as I walked into the infusion center at the hospital, I started complaining to the person who checked me in. Then, I complained to the nurse, and then to other people at the center. "Isn't it terrible I have to be here on my birthday?" I asked.

As I was moping around, my skills chart on the mirror at home popped into my head and I started thinking about gratitude. Halfway through the infusion, I had an epiphany. "Wait a minute," I thought, "What better place to celebrate my birthday than the place that gives me life?"

I began to feel genuinely happy to be there. I began to smile and thank the nurses for caring for me and express joy to my fellow "infusers." It was the same situation, just a different perspective — one unhappy, the other happy. One is a perspective of self-pity, the other a perspective of gratitude. The situation was no different, what changed was how I looked at it. Gratitude and happiness really are a choice.

How we choose to look at the past shapes how we look at the future and how we live in the present.

Compare the following two stories from my youth. Here's the first:

> *I was born in Schenectady, a desolate town in upstate New York that time seemed to forget. I was the youngest of four kids, all of them smarter and better at school than me. My dad worked for General Electric. He worked long hours and, while I am sure he loved me, he was short tempered and demanding. We moved a lot with his career. By the time I got settled into one town, we would move to another, including in the middle of my high school years. It*

was difficult for me to find new friends. For college, I attended DePauw, probably more because that's where my parents and sisters went than for any other reason. DePauw seemed far from everything I knew. It was in the middle of the cornfields of Indiana, in the unexciting town of Greencastle. I struggled with the adjustment to both college life and to my new surroundings. My childhood was difficult.

Here's the second:

I was born in Schenectady, New York, a town just south of the beautiful Adirondack Mountains. I was the youngest of four children. While I didn't do as well in school as they did, I think I was as capable — I was just interested in a hundred other things. My dad worked at General Electric, and though he was demanding and worked exceedingly hard, he loved, provided and cared for all of us kids, as did my mother. While he was full of challenge, my mom was full of acceptance and support. From that combination, I think my siblings and I had the courage to grow, explore and spread our wings as we reached adulthood. We moved a lot with my father's career, which gave me the opportunity to live in different areas of the country and discover their unique advantages. I went to DePauw, probably mostly because that is where my parents and sisters went, but it was a great place for me to grow and learn. I struggled to adjust during the first couple of years, but in the beginning of my junior year I met the love of my life. We have been married for 44 years. My childhood was blessed.

Both accounts are factually consistent, but they represent two very different perspectives on the same set of facts. The person who would relate the first story is very different from the person who would relate the second. Let me be more specific, the person who would relate the second story, which is full of gratitude, would be significantly happier and bring significantly greater joy to those around them.

Gratitude is the second skill regarding the past that leads to happiness.

Happiness is greatly influenced by the perspective we take, especially in how we choose to see our past. Do we see ourselves as victims of the circumstances we have experienced, or do we see ourselves as blessed by our circumstances? I will be the first to concede that the greater the number of negative or difficult circumstances a person endures, the harder it is to view the past as a blessing. But most of us have far more to be thankful for than we do to be angry or remorseful about, and those who are able to recognize this are considerably happier.

What influences how we feel about the past has less to do with our circumstances than the way we choose to view them. Here is a story I use in my class to illustrate this point:

Michael is a lawyer who lives on the east side of town. He is 35 years old, has two kids and has just bought a new BMW. He is driving across town and just happens to drift a few inches over the yellow line. Michelle is a lawyer who lives on the west side of town. She, too, is 35 years old, has two kids and has just bought a new BMW. As she drives in the opposite direction she too drifts a few inches over the yellow line.

Both cars are traveling 40 miles an hour (this is starting to sound like an algebra exam) when they collide head on. The cars skid to the side of the road. Michael gets out of his car, looks at his new BMW, which is now totaled, and can't believe this has happened to him. He lets out a few expletives, kicks the tires, realizes he will miss his important morning meeting and feels as if his day, probably his week, is ruined. He lets out a few more expletives and then pulls out his cell phone to tell others about his terrible misfortune.

Michelle, on the other hand, gets out of her car, looks over at Michael and sees he is not hurt, looks down at herself and realizes she is not hurt, and immediately thinks: "It's a miracle. I am standing here unhurt, no one else is hurt and I have just had a head on collision. It is a miracle! I can't believe it!" She pulls out her cell phone to tell others about her incredibly good fortune.

Life is more about perspectives than circumstances. So is happiness. Like forgiveness, gratitude is a mega-strategy of happiness. Forgiveness eliminates negatives. Gratitude magnifies positives. Put the two together and they can have a profound effect on our happiness.

Positive psychologists have done studies in which they have asked people to keep a gratitude journal. Specifically, they asked participants to take five minutes at the end of each day to write down three things for which they are grateful. After 30 days the participants are measurably happier, and if they keep this practice up their happiness level continues to rise.

Keeping a journal is actually a great tool for increasing our happiness by enabling us to relive past experiences that have brought us joy. In January 1986 while I was working at General Foods, we had a business meeting in Stowe, Vermont. Late one evening, I went for a long walk. It was a beautiful evening. When I came back I recorded the feelings I had in my journal:

It has snowed this day. The snow gently fell from the gray sky for much of the day onto land already turned white by previous snows. Only the dark green of the spruce and pine and hemlock poked through the gray and white world. The snow made no sound as it fell, yet it seemed to fill all my senses — filling me with a sense of belonging . . . a feeling that I was as much a part of the panorama as the snow, the trees and the massive mountains which surrounded me. My worth was measured by no more than merely being there. Nothing judged, or needing explanation, simply accepted as it is.

There is serenity in nature. I believe it is at the core of all of us. It is there from our ancestors from a thousand or ten thousand years back. To touch that core in us is to reach into the center of our being — of all being. To touch it brings a sense of fulfillment, of rest, of joy, of strength, of immense beauty and great understanding.

May God grant me the health to continue to touch this source of joy and the wisdom to value it again and again as I have on this bitterly cold day in January at the foot of Mount Mansfield.
—Author's journal, January 13, 1986

More than 25 years later I can look back at this journal entry and live that night over and over again, feeling the pleasure of that walk. In effect, I can multiply the pleasure associated with that past event by bringing it into the present and appreciating it whenever I choose.

Gratitude has been called the purest form of love because it asks nothing in return. It is simply an expression of appreciation. While it asks nothing in return, it brings happiness to whoever expresses it or feels it.

The first year I taught at DePauw as we talked about gratitude, one of the students raised her hand and said: "You know, I don't think I have ever told my parents how appreciative I am of them sending me to DePauw. I would like to call home and thank them tonight, but it would help if everyone else in the class would do the same."

Everyone in the class agreed to call home that night and to share the responses in class. The next morning I noticed that most of the students showed up about 15 minutes before the start of class, which had never happened before. I also noticed that almost all of them were smiling and more outgoing. The students then all shared what had happened when they called home. While many talked about their parents' responses, most of them ended up speaking about how good it had made them feel to express gratitude.

Some of the students' stories were hysterical. One student asked her mom to get dad on the phone. To which her mother replied, "Why?" When she asked again, her mother said, "Are you going to tell me something I don't want to hear? Are you pregnant?" The student replied, "No! Just get dad on the phone." When both parents were finally on the phone she spent three or four minutes explaining how appreciative she was for the opportunity to come to DePauw and the education they were providing her. When she finished there was a moment of silence, and then her mom asked, "Are you smoking something you shouldn't be?"

Since I started teaching, I have made it a practice to express appreciation to more and more people. I think it makes me happier to do so. Among the people I thank are the custodians who clean the buildings where I teach. I thank them when they clean the floors or the whiteboard. I have gotten to know them personally. In the past I wouldn't have done this, and now I am ashamed for not having done so.

I have also come to appreciate how much we can learn from others. One evening, while I was packing up to go, one of the custodians came in and looked at the whiteboard. He saw a quote by John Milton and said, "John Milton. He is one of my favorite English authors." "Really?" I said. He went on to give me a 15-minute lesson on John Milton. I learned a lot that evening.

More recently, I have started to express my appreciation for the people who keep the restrooms clean at airports and highway rest areas. Most are astounded that someone speaks to them. Many express appreciation and emphasize that they really do try to keep the rooms clean. Again, I am ashamed I took these folks for granted in the past.

Expressing gratitude is one of the easiest and simplest ways to increase happiness, and probably one of the least used. Each year, I ask my students how many of them wrote letters to Santa when they were little. Usually many, including me, had done so. I then ask if they had received what they asked for. Many, including me, had. I then ask them the telling question: "How many wrote Santa a thank you note?" No one, including me, had.

Here is another story I often use in class:

> *Bobby turns 16. On his birthday, he runs downstairs and out the front door to find in the driveway a Mercedes convertible with a bow around it and a note wishing him a happy birthday. Bobby walks once around the car and then runs upstairs to his parents' bedroom, rushes in and — brace yourself — says: "How come I got a Mercedes? I wanted a Porsche. Danny down the street got a Porsche!"*

We all probably have a similar response to this story: "What a spoiled, unappreciative brat!" But here is what I think we should all contemplate from this story: We each have been given a gift a million times more precious than the Mercedes, or even than the Porsche — the gift of life. How much of our time do we spend expressing appreciation and gratitude for that life versus complaining about the various trials and tribulations we face each day? Maybe, at times, we are more like Bobby than we would care to admit.

Several years ago Phyllis, the boys and I lived in Canada. We would frequently make the drive between Lake George and our home in Oakville, just west of Toronto. In summer we would often take a shortcut at the west end of the Adirondack Park that began at Big Moose Lake and ended in Lowville, New York. The shortcut involved traveling on an old dirt logging road that passed through miles of complete wilderness. For over 20 miles there were no houses, no businesses, no gas stations . . . nothing other than beautiful woods and mountains.

One January, when the temperature hovered around zero, I decided, over Phyllis's objections, to take the shortcut. As you might guess, this adventure did not end well. About 10 miles into the wilderness the car slipped off the dirt road into a snow bank. As darkness approached and we were contemplating what to do next, miraculously a group of snowmobilers came by. They helped us get the car out of the snow bank and turned around. One of the men who helped us commented that he had been snowmobiling on this road for over 10 years and had never seen a car back there. He then asked, "What possessed you to try this?" Phyllis rolled her eyes as I mumbled some weak explanation.

We drove out of the wilderness with the snowmobilers as escorts. As we continued to drive, Phyllis didn't remind me she had objected to taking the shortcut, or tell me how stupid I was, or even bring up the whole situation. She already knew I felt foolish and had learned a valuable lesson. She simply moved on. We eventually crossed into Canada just north of Buffalo late that night and I suggested we swing by Niagara Falls. As I stood there with my family gazing at the falls, I was filled with gratitude for so many things — the beauty of the falls, my dear family, for not being stuck in some snow bank deep in the wilderness, but perhaps most of all, for Phyllis's gracious ability to forgive.

Several months had passed by now in my journey to better practice the skills of happiness. To date I had focused on forgiveness and gratitude. That these two skills lead to happiness is simple arithmetic: forgiveness reduces the negative in our lives and gratitude magnifies the positive.

I thought I was making progress, but I also came to fully realize these 13 skills are ones we never master; hopefully, we just keep getting a little better at them as we age.

Finding happiness in the future is equally important to our happiness, but it requires a very different set of skills, so I decided I would turn my attention to the future.

Chapter 7

FACING THE FUTURE WITH CONFIDENCE

The gods have two ways of blessing us. One is to grant our wishes, the other is to deny them.
—Author, with apologies to Oscar Wilde

In the last chapter, I dealt with skills to finding peace about the past. The past is a key to happiness, not so much because that is where happiness is found, but because if we don't resolve feelings about events in our past, we can be so absorbed by remorse or anger that we fail to live in the present. Our past can screw up our future and our present if we don't find ways to resolve the complex web of feelings we have about it.

In this chapter, I will focus on how we find confidence in the future so that we don't face it with fear and trepidation, and miss the opportunity for happiness in the present. I will do this by sharing a story that I hope will be instructive.

After our silent trip to Minneapolis as newlyweds, Phyllis and I settled into a rented apartment. We loved the city, and I found my work at General Mills interesting and enjoyable. The summer passed quickly.

In the fall we moved to Sachem Village, the married-student housing at Dartmouth College in Hanover, New Hampshire, where I would finish my second year of Dartmouth's MBA program and Phyllis would teach sixth grade English in White River Junction, Vermont, 10 miles to the south.

I loved being married and I loved business school. I think I could have stayed at Dartmouth's business school for 10 years and never gotten bored. I thrived in business school.

Previously, school had always been about memorizing stuff, and memorization was not my strength. Much of the stuff we had to memorize seemed useless to me. In 8th grade, as a student in Hendersonville, North Carolina, I had to memorize the county seats of North Carolina's 100 counties. On the final exam, the counties were listed down the left side of the page and we were to fill in the county seats on the right. Perhaps at some point in my life that knowledge will come in handy, but it hasn't happened yet. I do recall that the county seat of Henderson County is Hendersonville, where I lived. At least I got one right.

But business school, at least at Dartmouth, wasn't about memorizing useless stuff. In fact, it wasn't about memorizing stuff at all. It was about concepts and ideas; it was about real life situations, problems and opportunities. Much of the learning and teaching was based on the case method, where our challenge was to understand the dilemma faced by a business leader and figure out how to capitalize on the opportunity or solve the problem using the concepts learned in class. Additionally, students do most of their work in teams, which suited me well.

I lived in the mountains of New Hampshire. Dartmouth had a beautiful campus and its own ski mountain 15 minutes up Route 10. I got to work in teams. I was married. I didn't have to memorize the county seats of New Hampshire. Business school was nirvana.

But business school did have to end, so in February 1970 I started the interviewing process that eventually led to my joining General Foods, in White Plains, New York. In August, Phyllis and I moved to nearby New Canaan, Connecticut. Phyllis worked at the New Canaan Bookstore and I drove 22 miles down the Merritt Parkway to General Foods, where I was an assistant product manager on Tang Instant Breakfast Drink, the one that went to the moon.

In December, Phyllis discovered she was pregnant. For the next seven months Phyllis did everything you should do to have a "successful" pregnancy and a healthy baby. She ate well, didn't drink alcohol, didn't smoke, and didn't over-exercise or otherwise participate in activities that would put her pregnancy at risk. She read voraciously about pregnancy and delivery.

On Friday evening July 9, 1971, we had dinner with close friends and then went to the movies. We saw *Little Big Man* starring Dustin Hoffman and Faye Dunaway, then went home and went to bed. After midnight Phyllis woke up with stomach pains. We didn't think too much about it until around 2 a.m. when they seemed to get progressively worse. We called the obstetrician's emergency number and he suggested we go to Greenwich Hospital where he practiced.

An hour later, at 3 a.m. Saturday morning, the doctor pronounced that Phyllis had placenta separation, when the placenta separates from the wall of the uterus, and that our baby had an elevated heart rate and was in distress. I didn't even know what "placenta separation" meant, but I put the future of my wife and child in his hands. He said it was necessary to perform a cesarean section. Gordon was born one month premature around 4 a.m. and placed into the nursery with the other newborns. Phyllis and I were elated. We were exhausted, but relieved that we had made it through the night and that we had a baby boy to begin expanding our family. Before sunrise, I headed home thinking everything was fine.

Within hours, Gordon experienced difficulty breathing, as his lungs were not fully developed. We soon learned the doctor had misdiagnosed placenta separation, and whether the nurses on duty were as attentive to Gordon as they should have been, we will never know. Much of his birth is, and will remain, a mystery. What we do know is that Gordon's breathing difficulties had a permanent effect on his development and his capabilities, and this would in turn lead me on a 40-year lesson in happiness. (I can be a little slow.)

In the months after we brought Gordon home, we realized that his development might be slowed because of his difficulties during birth. He rolled over after a few weeks, which we thought was a good sign. It wasn't. Children with developmental difficulties often roll over sooner than normal babies because of stiffness in their movement.

Gordon was slow to crawl, and when he did, he moved both of his arms at once, rather than alternating hands — another sign of developmental difficulties. Gordon didn't walk until he was 2 years old and his talking lagged far behind other kids his age. During this time we became increasingly aware that Gordon would not have "normal" capabilities.

While Phyllis seemed to grasp this better than I did, we both struggled to accept Gordon as he was, often wishing he could be like so many of our friends' children, moving through the stages of development at a "normal" pace. Instead of loving Gordon for who he was and taking joy in each of his developmental steps, I kept comparing him to others and wishing the situation was different. In many ways I moved to "Pity City," complaining and bemoaning the fact that Gordon's development wasn't normal. I loved Gordon and enjoyed many things about him, but deep down I was angry that Gordon wasn't like other kids.

Phyllis devoted herself to raising Gordon, optimizing his growth and taking care of me and our home. She eventually found other parents of children with special needs in our community and they formed a special parents group to advocate for special-needs kids and share the struggles of raising them. I, instead, let my imagination run wild. I thought, "He'll never be able to walk," until he walked. Then, "He'll never be able to talk," until he talked. And on it went.

We waited six years before contemplating having another child. In May 1978, our second son Greg was born by cesarean section at full term and with no difficulties.

Greg was at the other end of the development spectrum, reaching stages at normally anticipated times. I had the privilege of coaching his little league baseball team, playing in tennis tournaments with him, and making ski trips with him. He excelled in school, eventually attending Middlebury College in Vermont, graduating with high honors, working at Unilever for three years, and then going to graduate school and earning his MBA at my alma mater, Dartmouth's Tuck School of Business. He is very entrepreneurial and has recently stepped out on his own, doing consulting work in business planning and finance. Greg is bright, funny, independent, spirited and responsible. He works hard and is a joy to both Phyllis and me.

I am not sure when it was, but sometime during Gordon's early teenage years, I started to look at Gordon differently.

I gradually stopped comparing him to other people. I released my fear and trepidation about what the future would hold and began to accept him for who he was and what he could do. By statistical measures, Gordon probably has an IQ (intelligence quotient) just shy of 60. However, what Gordon lacks in IQ, he more than makes up for with his EQ (emotional quotient).

No matter what Phyllis and I are doing, Gordon almost always says, "I'll help you," and he does. He relates very well with others. He cares about others and expresses that care effectively and often. Because we lived outside of Toronto while he was growing up, he attended special classes in public school until he was 21. Canadians devote more time and attention to those with special needs than we do in the United States. Much of his schooling was devoted to vocational training. In Canada he worked at a Food City grocery store.

For the past 17 years he has worked as a bagger at a Kroger grocery store in Columbus, Ohio, where we now live. Kroger hires a lot of people with special needs and for that we are deeply grateful. Other corporations could learn a lot from how Kroger helps and capitalizes on the skills of people with special needs. Most interesting to me is how the practice benefits all stakeholders, including Kroger's associates, customers and investors — not just the special-needs employees. It is a win/win decision for everyone associated with Kroger.

Gordon lives with us in a suite of rooms over our garage. He and Greg are both incredible blessings in our lives, but how I came to see Gordon in this manner is a lesson in how we think about the future and, therefore, happiness.

I tend to judge everything and everyone. It is a lousy habit. When I meet someone, I assign attributes to them, such as fat, skinny, tall, short, smart, dumb, young, old, attractive, unattractive, grumpy, happy, funny, stiff, outgoing, etc. And then I add a perspective that this is either good or bad. I do the same with events. Everything that happens to me I immediately judge as either good or bad, and Gordon's difficulties from birth were no exception. But the truth is we often can't tell whether something that happens is good or bad.

Gordon has turned out to be one of the most incredible joys of Phyllis's and my life. Who knew? Because Gordon is my son, I believe I have become a better person — one who understands, appreciates and cherishes life so much more fully. And, hopefully, I am more accepting and kind.

Our second son Greg has been an equally incredible blessing, which reminds me that the Gods really do have two ways of blessing us: one is to grant our wishes and the other is to deny them. Gordon's developmentally challenged birth has been as much a blessing to Phyllis and me as the birth of our second son Greg. Yes, they are different and bring with them different challenges, but they each are a source of happiness in their own way. I realized that after years of self-pity.

Life is full of hundreds of surprises or mysteries daily. Instead of judging each one, I now try to accept them and make them my friend. What I have come to understand, is that as we face the future, we have to learn to "marry the mystery" of life.

Most of us approach the future by looking ahead and thinking that if we do this, then this desired outcome should occur. Sort of like this:

I am here... If I do this... I expect to get here.

In many ways this is healthy. When we want something we act in a particular way to bring it about. The world would be a sad place if we didn't look to the future and act in a way that serves to bring a desired result. However, the model we have in our head is too simple and fixed. We almost always see one, and only one, pathway forward. In effect, we tend to think we can control the future with our actions.

In truth, the second we step into the future, it will almost always be different than the future we assumed. The future will seldom unfold exactly as we have envisioned. When the world moves forward in a way that is different than we envisioned, we suddenly are knocked off track and think, "This is bad!"

What I am trying to learn is to accept that the future will be different than what I envision. I try not to judge the variations, but instead ask what I can do to get back on a pathway that will lead me where I want to be. There are an infinite number of ways the future could unfold and still take us to where we want to go. Much of the stress we feel in life, I believe, comes from the rigid concept we have of the future and our inability to deal with the myriad diversions the future will always bring.

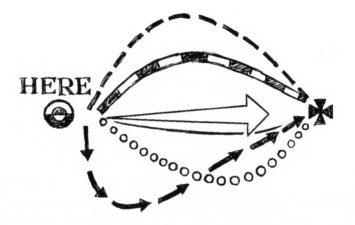

But an even deeper lesson to learn is that as the future unfolds, despite our best efforts, the pathway forward may not only be different, but where it eventually leads may be different. It may never lead to where we originally envisioned. It may take us to any number of different destinations. And that may be just fine. The end point may be very different than the one we envisioned, but it still may hold promise:

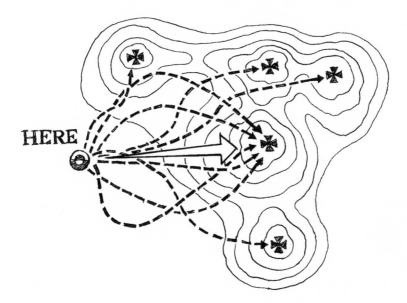

I have come to realize that if we do our part, the universe will do its part and bring us what we need — not necessarily what we want, but always what we need. If we do our part, things will work to our advantage. Seneca said, "If one does not know to which port one is sailing, no wind is favorable." Perhaps the converse is also true: If you *know* where you are going, *all* wind is favorable.

When Gordon was born, Phyllis had done everything she could to have a particular outcome come true. As is often the case, the universe had a different course. Rather than bemoan that our life turned out differently than planned, we needed to accept what had happened and then figure out how to move from there. When we encounter setbacks in life we often go through a grieving process. This process is healthy. The first step of that process is not acceptance, but that is where it hopefully leads.

Many factors stand between where we are today and the future outcome we desire. And many of those we can't control. The future is almost always different than what we expect. It is healthy to desire something and act in a particular way to bring it about. What is not healthy is failing to realize that we don't control the future.

I have learned over and over that if I do my part, the universe will always work in my favor, but it will do so on its agenda, not on mine. Gordon isn't the son I envisioned before he was born, but he is an incredible son. In fact, now he is an incredible young man of 42. If I had "married the mystery," I wouldn't have spent so many years in "Pity City."

I know that major setbacks often require considerable time to accept. For new parents, accepting that their child will be developmentally disabled can be a long, lonely, difficult task. I also recognize there is a natural progression of stages we pass through in dealing with a major setback. Elizabeth Kubler-Ross identified these as denial, anger, bargaining, depression and acceptance. But the happiest among us move through these early stages rather than making them permanent places of residence.

Phyllis's and my focus has shifted from "poor us" and what Gordon can't do, to marveling at what he does achieve, helping him develop to his full potential and enjoying him for the fine young man he is. As I look back, I am embarrassed that so much of my prior focus was on how Gordon's handicap would affect me, and so little on what it must be like for him to face the challenges of life. I am glad I am in a different spot today, even if the struggle to get here was long and difficult.

"Marrying the mystery" goes beyond accepting negative news or "making lemonade out of lemons." It is not viewing the things that happen to us as necessarily negative, or lemons. In *Are You Ready to Succeed,* Srikumar Rao recounts an ancient Sufi tale, which I will abbreviate.

A peasant sells all of his worldly possessions and buys a beautiful stallion. The first night he has the stallion, it jumps the fence and runs away. All his neighbors come and say, "What bad news," to which he responds, "Good news, bad news — who knows?" Two weeks later the stallion comes back with 10 mares. The neighbors come over and say, "What good news!" And he responds, "Good news, bad news — who knows?" A week later, his son goes out to break the stallion and falls off, breaking his leg in many places and leaving him crippled.

The neighbors' comments and the peasant's responses continue in the same vein. Then there is a war and the king calls up all able-bodied men, but the son cannot go. All of those called up die, but the son lives. The cycle continues.

When events occur, we really don't know whether it's good news or bad news, so we ought to stop guessing and just accept the news as reality, then move on.

"Marrying the mystery" is not easy. I am working to develop a set of skills that will help me do this more consistently. I have an acronym for them: **FOFO**, for Faith, Optimism, Flexibility and Openness.

Faith

The first skill is faith. A lot of things are not possible without faith, happiness among them. By faith I mean confidence and trust in the future. In effect, someone with faith has a higher likelihood of feeling that no matter what the future brings, they will figure out a way to deal with it. Faith can conquer fear.

Faith, or trust and confidence in the future, can come from a number of sources, including religion, or a belief that some larger force is caring for us. But however we come by faith, it is essential to happiness. Without faith, our imagination conjures up all kinds of terrible scenarios, potential setbacks and tragedies. The more vivid our imagination, the worse the scenarios we spin.

Shakespeare wrote in *Othello*, "Imagination without faith is a cruel master." It is through faith that we rein in our imagination. The happiest people among us don't have a lot of fear about the future because they have faith or confidence in their ability to deal with whatever the future may hold.

Optimism

The ability to face the future with confidence also comes from optimism. We each have the ability to think optimistically or pessimistically. I think most pessimism is a waste of time. Whenever I slip into a pessimistic mood, I know it doesn't serve me well. One of my favorite children's books, *The Little Engine that Could*, by Watty Piper, illustrated it well: Optimism powers us forward. When my business partners and I faced a devastating piece of news about 10 years ago, my wife bought me a copy of the book. We are never too old for some messages.

Some people suggest that pessimism spurs them on; that by being pessimistic, they are being more realistic. I don't buy it. Research actually shows that the more optimistic we are, the more we will persist in the face of adversity. As Eisenhower said, "I never met a pessimistic general who ever won a battle."

We all seem to register the benefits of optimism in sports, but many of us fail to translate those benefits to life in general. If we want to sink a putt, throw a three-pointer, hit a solid backhand shot, hit a homerun, hit a drive down the center of the fairway, we all advocate visualizing success, not failure. When we translate that same positive visualization to life, many of us think of it as being Pollyanna-ish.

However we choose to think, we all have a tendency to look for information, situations and facts that will confirm how we visualize the world. If we have a negative or pessimistic view, we look for data to confirm that viewpoint. My son Greg informed me the other day that there is even a phrase in scientific research for this: "confirmation bias." In other words, think pessimistically and you will see the world in a way that confirms that negative view. See the world with optimism, and you will see all kinds of positive confirmation.

I am not suggesting that foolish optimism is appropriate. It isn't. Foolish optimism can kill you, as in: "I can drink and drive, and it will be fine"; or "I can eat anything I want and not have heart disease"; or "I don't really need to get a colonoscopy since the one I had 10 years ago was fine."

I am also not suggesting that we sit around and think positive thoughts and wait for something good to happen. To the contrary, the happiest among us are both optimistic and devoted to bringing their optimistic visions to fruition. Can you imagine Edmund Hillary thinking, "I will never be able to climb Everest"; or Roger Bannister thinking, "I will never break the four-minute mile"; or Herb Brooks thinking, "We will never beat the Soviet hockey team"—and any of them still achieving the success they did?

Like happiness, genetics plays a role in our ability to be optimistic. But before you think optimism is something other than a skill, consider that Martin Seligman's central message in *Learned Optimism* details how we can develop the skill of optimism. Like happiness, optimism is a skill that some of us are better at than others, but it is nonetheless a skill that can be developed and enhanced.

Seligman and others in the field of positive psychology conclude that optimists and pessimists think about events in very different manners. When optimists confront an obstacle, they tend to think of it as temporary, specific to that event and something that they can correct. An optimistic student who gets a bad grade on a test might think: "It is just one test. I probably didn't study as hard as I needed to, and if I really focus I will do fine on the next test."

In contrast, pessimists tend to think of setbacks as pervasive, permanent and something over which they have little or no control. After failing a test, a pessimistic student would be more likely to think: "I am stupid. I am not up to college work. I will probably not do well in my other courses either."

When a positive event occurs, the roles are reversed. The optimist assigns more permanence and broad relevance to the good event, and the pessimist thinks it is more temporary and specific to the event.

Pessimism is really a form of fear, and the more we use fear as a motivator, the more fearful we become. Fear and happiness are not good companions. In fact, left unchecked, fear will devour happiness. Motivating ourselves to meet the challenges we face each day through fear and pessimism may have some positive consequences, but it is a cheap trick because it robs us of the happiness we so richly deserve. As 14th century Iranian poet Hafiz said: "Fear is the cheapest room in the house. I would like to see you living in better conditions."

Flexibility and Openness

The last two traits I am working to develop are flexibility and openness. I am trying to be flexible in how I respond to situations and open to new pathways and new destinations. Helen Keller said: "When one door of happiness closes, another opens; but often we look so long at the closed door that we do not see the one which has opened for us."

I have my blood tested every two weeks or so. It is called a complete blood count, or CBC. I have gotten pretty good at being able to interpret the results. The measures include white blood cell counts and what percentage of those white blood cells are lymphocytes versus neutrophils. The count also includes hemoglobin and red blood cells, and for me, the biggie, platelets. I know what is considered normal for all of these, and I am able to watch the trends.

I used to get the results, and if the platelets were down, I would think, "Oh no, this is not good." If the neutrophils were up, I'd think, "Oh, this is good." I am looking at them differently now. They are what they are. Who knows? Platelets being down could be good news. It could mean that I move more quickly to some experimental medicine that works miraculously. Who knows?

The point is we simply don't know whether something is good news or bad news. What I am trying to do is accept the news in a more neutral way, and do everything I can to live a healthy life that doesn't damage my ability to make healthy blood cells. I want to be more flexible and open to new pathways, to face the future with the belief that no matter what happens I will find a light, a path, a door that enables me to move forward. I am not there yet, but I am working on it.

Together faith, optimism, flexibility and openness, or **FOFO**, are powerful skills that enable us to have confidence in the future. If I could possess and practice these skills consistently, I think I would be happier. My guess is this would be true for all of us.

I want to share one last story about my son Gordon, with whom I opened this chapter. There is an innocence about Gordon that is really quite charming and special. You wouldn't find it in most 42 year olds, and it is a gift most parents don't enjoy with grown children. At bedtime, he still likes for me to tell him a story. I use a little hand puppet. It's a wolf named, quite creatively, "Mr. Wolf." Most nights before he heads to bed, I tell him a Mr. Wolf story.

I also told Greg Mr. Wolf stories, but he outgrew them. Now, there are hundreds of other wonderful ways Greg and I relate as adults. We have conversations that range from politics, to investing and finance, to world events, to family concerns. We have the dialogues many adults have. It is a joy to share these with him.

My conversations with Gordon are different. They are no less rewarding, meaningful, or enjoyable — just different. We talk about sports and his work, we both love music and have similarly programmed iPods — and we have Mr. Wolf stories. The fact that he hasn't outgrown these stories, in many ways, is a gift.

Gordon's innocence is evident in other endearing ways. We were taking our morning walk some months ago and a very attractive woman stepped out of her house and said, "Hi, Gordon." To which he responded, "Good morning, Mrs. Miller." We walked on about another 50 yards, then Gordon leaned over and said to me in a soft voice, "I bagged Mrs. Miller." I said, "You what?" Gordon replied, "I bagged Mrs. Miller at Kroger."

I then understood he was talking about Mrs. Miller's groceries. I felt an incredible sense of joy as I considered the common, more crass and sexist meaning of his statement and his innocence in uttering it. I still smile every time I think of this incident.

Gordon is an incredible gift that brings joy to Phyllis and me each day. Greg is an equally beautiful gift. If I was still agonizing about what Gordon can't do and hadn't come to appreciate and accept him just as he is — if I hadn't learned to face the future with a certain level of faith, optimism, flexibility and openness, or **FOFO** — I would miss so much joy.

I am eternally grateful for Gordon, Greg and my wife — just the way they are.

Chapter 8

LIVING IN THE PRESENT WITH JOY

At any moment the fully present mind can shatter time and burst into Now.
—David Steindl-Rast

If happiness is found in the present, then why did I spend the last two chapters dealing with the past and the future? I did so for the simple reason that many of us, including me, have spent inordinate amounts of our lives in anguish over the past or worrying about the future, thereby missing the opportunities for joy in the present.

Most of us are familiar with the concept of "choking" in sports. I think it would be fair to say that choking happens the second we step out of the present and into the past with anger or remorse, or step into the future with fear.

Several months ago I was playing golf on my home course of Tartan Fields in Dublin, Ohio. I had never broken 80 on the course. This particular Saturday I arrived at the 16th hole three over par. I proceeded to four putt the 16th green, and then to put my ball in the water on the short par 3 number 17. I was then seven over par. As I stood on the 18th tee, I realized I must get a par on the hole or I would blow my chance to break 80. I could feel the anger and remorse I had about the last two holes, and my mind raced forward to consider what would happen if I hit my drive into the woods here on 18. I was choking. I was stepping out of the present and into the past with remorse and anger, at the same time I was stepping into the future with fear.

I didn't break 80, but I learned — and continue to learn — a key lesson of happiness: the importance of living in the present. In sports stepping out of the present with feelings of anger or remorse about the past or fear about the future is called "choking." In life, it is called "unhappiness."

The skills covered in the last two chapters enable us to be at peace with the past and to have confidence about the future, which in turn frees us to LIVE in the present. In this chapter, I want to share a set of skills that enable us to live with joy and exuberance in the present, to find happiness in the present. Practicing these skills consistently is a lifelong endeavor. Do not be discouraged if you are less than perfect at practicing any of them. I struggle every day with these seven skills, as well as the skills of the past and the future covered earlier. I think I am getting better — and therefore happier — but perfection in this, as in golf, is not possible for anyone.

Doing Now What I Am Doing Now

Yesterday is ashes, tomorrow wood. Only today the
fire burns brightly.
—Eskimo saying

In early 2007 I was about 12 months into my journey of learning to practice the skills of happiness. On a beautiful winter night in February, I rediscovered one of the keys to living in the present with joy.

When we lived in Canada we had a fireplace in our master bedroom. It was wonderful. I think of it as a "marital aid." It was very romantic. In 1996 we moved to Columbus, Ohio. The house we found lacked only one thing: a fireplace in the master bedroom. I shudder to think how much it eventually ended up costing us, but we now have a fireplace in our master bedroom.

On a very cold winter night in February as the snow was falling outside, Phyllis and I were settled into our canopy bed with a fire roaring in the fireplace at the foot of the bed. Phyllis was sharing some of the things that had happened during the day, and as I laid back, relaxed and watched the fire, I could hear the wind outside rustling the shutters. I thought how lucky I was to be in here, where it was warm and comfortable. The day's worries and challenges seemed far away. I could almost feel my heart rate slow, my blood pressure decline and a state of grace come over me.

After five or 10 minutes as the conversation slowed, I reached over for my computer by the side of the bed and began to search through the Internet. I also turned on the TV to hear the late night news. I still had my cell phone handy, so I whipped off a few text messages about a meeting the following day. The newspaper had an interesting story, so I began scanning the article. Pretty soon I was involved in about four different activities, and all the while I was "listening" to an occasional observation from Phyllis. I was thinking I could do all of these things at once because I was really good at multi-tasking. There was only one problem: I was doing none of them well. As I was multi-tasking I could feel my pulse and blood pressure rising, not to mention Phyllis's. I used to pride myself on the ability to multi-task. I now recognize it is a big robber of happiness.

This leads us to the first skill for living with joy in the present... be there! Or as someone once said to me, "Do now what you are doing now." The present is dripping with opportunities for joy and happiness, but you have to be present to enjoy the present.

"Doing now what you are doing now" means being present in the moment. The first key is to stop multitasking. Do one thing at a time and do that one thing well.

At Phyllis's suggestion, we no longer have a TV in our bedroom. We no longer choose to bring our computers, cell phones or newspapers into the bedroom. Our master bedroom is for resting, reading and relationship. If you want to lower your blood pressure and enjoy your time together in the bedroom, add a fireplace or light a candle or two. Remove the TV and other distractions.

Sometime ago, I was helped in my career by Judy Marcus, a business consultant in Greenwich, Connecticut. She was quick to pick up on my excessive multi-tasking. She helped me be present in the moment with a technique she called "thresholds." She said, "Doug, I want you to start thinking about every door you pass through as a threshold, and in so doing I want you to concentrate on where you are, not where you have been or where you will be. For instance, when you go home tonight, I want you to think about the doorway that goes from the garage into the house as a 'threshold.' As you pass through that doorway, or threshold, I want you to concentrate fully on what is happening on that side of the threshold, or what is happening in the house, and not what you have left behind — the traffic, the mess at the office, the news you heard on the radio, etc. I want you to focus solely on what is happening where you are, at home."

I said, "But often I need to do office work at home." She responded: "That's fine. You have an office or study at home, so pass through that doorway, or threshold, and work there. Your family will know that is where you need to focus on work. What I don't want you to do is do your work at home while talking to your kids, having dinner, talking with your wife. I want you to focus on where you are. Likewise, here at work I want you to focus on one thing at a time. When you go into a meeting room, I want you to focus on what is going on in the meeting, not something that you have to do later in the day, or the things that happened yesterday, or last week. Focus on where you are."

As I reflected back on the cold night in February and my tendency to multi-task, I realized I needed to get back to my "thresholds" concept and focus on where I was at the moment.

Ironically, as I write this there is an article on the front page of the *New York Times* about the proliferation of screens people are using so they can keep track of email, text messages, blogs, news, stock quotes, Facebook updates, tweets and video games. Sounds like a heart attack in waiting. The article explains that many people have three or more screens they are keeping track of at any given time as they work.

One man says he works off of six screens at once. Another woman, who typically has three screens up, says that having a single screen would be like going back to the rotary phone. She explains, "I don't want to miss anything." But she is missing something — she is missing the present. And the guy with six screens doesn't even know where to look for the present.

If you have ever tried meditation, you know how difficult it is to simply be present in the moment. Most of us who are not experts in meditation find that our mind wanders very quickly from the present moment. I know I am wired with "monkey brain," which means my brain loves to hop from one place and time to another. Meditation is powerful because it enables me to be fully in the present. There are many kinds of meditation practices, but central to them all is getting the participant to slow down, concentrate on the present, and release the thoughts about the past and the future. It has been shown that practicing meditation has numerous benefits in terms of dealing with stress, lowering blood pressure, increasing creativity and enabling better presence of mind. In other words, it is a great way to increase our happiness.

Pleasure can be one of the best parts of living in the present and can be a key source of happiness. Unfortunately, we can also misuse pleasure to our detriment, which we will discuss in the next chapter. But in this chapter, I want to talk about ways to increase the level of pleasure we get from everyday activities by being increasingly present.

Have you ever watched professional wine tasters? There is a very elaborate procedure around the task of sampling a wine. They start with the cork. They examine it and then they sniff it. They pour a little wine in the glass. They swirl the wine around in the glass. They look at its color; they look at its "tear," or how it runs down the side of the glass. Then they sniff the wine two or three times.

Finally, they taste the wine. But they don't just drink the wine; they take it into their mouth in a very specific way so that it coats the top of their mouth. They think about how it tastes on their tongue, the top and sides of their mouth and, as they swallow, what type of "finish" it has. They contemplate all the different flavors the wine has. Does it taste of black cherry, cinnamon, or artichoke? OK, maybe you can tell I don't know what I am talking about with wine, but I don't think I'm too far off in terms of the concentration and focus that wine tasters put into the process of evaluating a wine.

I think there is a lot to be learned from the wine taster. The wine taster is savoring, spacing and being very mindful of the pleasure of drinking a glass of wine. The wine taster is incredibly present. We have the opportunity to do the same with the various pleasures we experience as well.

Much of life is mindless, meaning that we don't focus on the here and now. We aren't present, but drift around from the past to the future to anyplace but here in the present. The wine taster is present, and is, in fact, relishing the present. We can follow the wine taster's lead when we eat a simple meal, relish a sunset, or enjoy sitting by a fire.

Let's start with savoring. Savoring is simply focusing our attention on the pleasure at hand. When eating a bowl of ice cream, many of us wolf it down, never taking the time to really think about what we are doing. Slowing down our eating — thinking about the taste, the texture, the sensation of the ice cream on our tongues, the smell and the feel — are ways to heighten the pleasure of the experience.

In other words, taking something we find pleasurable and breaking the process of doing it into many pieces is a way to heighten our enjoyment. Next time you have a bowl of ice cream, try taking a bite and then putting the spoon down and not taking another bite for one minute. OK, no one can do that (especially if it is from Jeni's Splendid Ice Creams), but how about waiting 30 seconds? What you are doing is giving your mind and body the time to fully appreciate the pleasure of eating ice cream, versus consuming ice cream while your mind is someplace else.

Part of the experience described above is the idea of spacing, or putting time between the points of stimuli. Pleasure comes from an outside stimulus. In particular, it comes from the change in stimuli. We don't respond to a steady stream of stimuli with as much pleasure as we do when the stimuli are spread out over a longer period of time. Putting more time between whatever stimulus we find pleasurable is an excellent way to increase the amount of pleasure we receive.

So far we have talked about ways to heighten bodily pleasure. Positive psychologists talk about another kind of pleasure they call "higher-order pleasure." This may or may not entail bodily pleasure, but it requires more thinking to experience. Sitting by a warm fire on a cold winter night reading a book is an example of higher-order pleasure. So are watching a sunset or moonrise over a distant mountain, or contemplating the satisfaction of having your baby or grandbaby wrap its hand around your little finger. These pleasures are ones we enjoy more by "doing now what I am doing now."

Often with higher-order pleasures, we can extend the pleasure they bring us by sharing the experience with others, or taking photographs that remind us time and again how the experience felt. Journaling is a particularly powerful means of capturing and reliving the experience of a higher-order pleasure.

"Do now what you are doing now." If you multitask a lot, figure out how to stop. Most important, give other people your full attention when speaking with them. My wife is a master at this. I still remember the attribute that most endeared me to her when I met her all those years ago was that she gave me her undivided attention. It was as if what I had to say was really important, which it wasn't. But she was present in the moment, and I loved her for it.

When others are speaking most of us let our minds wander in a hundred different directions. I think I know why. Researchers suggest that our minds can handle about 140 bits of information a second. Casual conversation requires about 40 bits of information a second. So when someone else is speaking to us, we basically have 100 bits of information that is free to do other things. Wow! We can use that to think about what will happen later in the day, reminisce about something that happened months ago, watch TV, read the newspaper, daydream . . . the possibilities are endless. But consider this — if we take all of our 140 bits of information capability and really listen, it can have a profound effect on us and those with whom we interact. People want to be appreciated, perhaps more than anything. Next time someone is speaking to you, try giving them 100 percent of your attention, focusing all 140 bits of information capability on them, and see what happens.

In October 2011, Phyllis, Gordon and I were planning to head to the Homestead in Virginia for a week's vacation. A couple of days before we were scheduled to leave, Phyllis got a sore throat and a bad cold. When she realized she could not go, she suggested Gordon and I go for the week. A day later, he and I were making the six-hour car ride from Ohio.

For a week, I did what Gordon did. We would wake up, have breakfast, then go for a long hike. Then we would have lunch together, and after lunch we would go golfing — Gordon driving the cart and putting when we got to the greens — or we would bowl, or go to the library in the hotel if it was raining. We would then go out to dinner, after which we would watch on TV whatever he was interested in.

For seven days, I focused only on being in the present and on Gordon. I was giving Gordon all 140 bits of my information capability. I was "doing now what I am doing now." I am sure Gordon enjoyed the week, but for me it was an incredible joy. I will remember and cherish that week forever.

When we talk about happiness in the present at the DePauw class, I invite a visitor named Professor Norton. Professor Norton is an expert on living in the present. He doesn't have any remorse about the past. He doesn't agonize about how he treated the neighbor's cat last week or the fact that he recently had an accident on the carpet. And he doesn't worry about the future, wondering where he'll get his next meal or if he will have time to play with some of his friends.

He doesn't worry about any of these things because Professor Norton is my son Greg's dog. If you could ask Professor Norton what time it is, I am sure he would respond: *"It's now! What time is it? Don't you understand? It's NOW! It's NOW!"*

We have some very real advantages compared to Professor Norton. We can learn from the past and we can anticipate and plan for the future, but much of the time we misuse these capabilities, agonizing about what happened long

PROFESSOR NORTON

ago and excessively worrying about what will happen in the future.

Being present in the present is powerful in that it leads to greater happiness. Ask yourself how much time you spend in the present compared to time spent agonizing about the future or the past. Enjoy thoughts about the past and plan for the future, but LIVE in the present. It is where real joy is found.

Honoring Our Mind, Body and Spirit

To what and to whom do you give access to your mind and body?
—Dennis Bland,
Center for Leadership Development

My good friend Dennis Bland graduated from DePauw University and went on to get his law degree at Indiana University. He then began a career at a law firm in Indianapolis. Dennis wanted to serve his community, and because he had benefitted from an organization called Center for Leadership Development (CLD) as a high school student, he decided he would offer his services as a member of its board of advisors.

CLD is a nonprofit organization devoted to helping the inner-city youth of Indianapolis find their way to successful adult lives by connecting them with educational and career opportunities. At any given time, it has about 2,500 students, ranging in age from 4 to 18, enrolled in evening and weekend classes.

Dennis had been involved on the board for several years, when the CLD needed a new executive director. When asked to take the job, he gave up his successful law practice to do so.

Dennis has a question he repeatedly asks of his students: "To what and to whom do you give access to your mind and your body?" I think it is a question we all need to ask ourselves, repeatedly.

Let's start with the **"what"**. When I got married in 1969, I weighed 150 pounds. Phyllis and I moved to Minneapolis for the summer and I began a job working for General Mills on Bisquick Baking Mix. I spent many afternoons tasting and learning about various new recipes for dinners or desserts one could make with Bisquick. The test dishes were all prepared by the culinary experts in the Betty Crocker Kitchen.

Meanwhile back home, my wife was enjoying cooking. She made wonderful meals for dinner each evening, complete with delicious desserts. I often came home from the office full, and then my wife would set another meal before me. I didn't want to disappoint her, so I ate it all. Some nights I would have to say, "Just let me just lie down on the couch for a few minutes before dessert."

We didn't have a scale because we were renting a furnished apartment for the summer. My boss invited us to his home one Saturday night, and when I went into their bathroom during the evening, I noticed a scale and stepped on it.

Pretty soon I was completely naked in my boss's bathroom tipping the scales at nearly 170 pounds. I had gained nearly 20 pounds in about 10 weeks of marriage. I began to calculate: Let's see — at this rate I will weigh 320 pounds by year's end!

When we got home that night, Phyllis and I discussed my weight gain. She agreed to not make dessert and I decided to limit my tasting at work. I was slowly learning to take responsibility for what I was giving access to my body.

In *Compass of Pleasure,* David Linden suggests that if we leave it to the food companies to decide what we give access to our body, we will be very disappointed with the results. Food companies have figured out that sugar and fat light up the pleasure circuits of our brains. And when they put sugar and fat together and give us lots of it, it lights those pleasure centers even more, or as he puts it, it's "superaddictive."

Food companies also know that if we don't have to chew a whole lot — think chicken nuggets — we eat more. Add contrasting flavors — think spicy chicken nuggets and cool ranch sauce — and give us huge or unlimited quantities, and we are in heaven.

David Linden further reveals that the average American weighs 26 pounds more today than in 1960. We are not taller or stronger; we are just carrying around 26 more pounds of fat. Ever seen a picture of what 5 pounds of human fat looks like? It is not pretty, and 26 pounds looks a lot worse. We are redesigning airplane seats, chairs, clothes and bathtubs to accommodate how much fatter we have become as a society.

More than 35 percent of Americans are obese. It doesn't have to be that way. In Japan, only 3.5 percent of the population is obese. Obesity is a major factor in shortening life expectancy. And frighteningly, obesity is rapidly increasing among America's youth. The percentage of obese kids has more than doubled in the last 30 years. The health consequences and costs to our society because of this weight gain are immense.

Of course, food is just the tip of the iceberg when it comes to the items that we give access to our bodies. Tobacco, alcohol and drugs can wreak far more havoc than food and make happiness a distant memory. We'll cover these items in more detail later, but suffice it to say that being fully conscious of what we put in our bodies is a key to finding happiness.

There are numerous books on, and resources for, healthy eating, but the point I want to make is that controlling the items we give access to our body is an important step to happiness. I know that many of us find keeping our weight in a normal range exceedingly difficult. For much of our existence as a species we struggled to get enough to eat, and this has left us with a strong preference for high-calorie and high-fat foods. But this skill is one that is well worth developing and nurturing.

The second half of Dennis's guiding question to the youths of CLD is "to **whom** do we give access?" Who do we choose to be with, to have as friends? Going further, what do we watch on TV, what music do we listen to, what websites do we visit, what do we read, and what parties do we go to? Whom and what are we letting into our minds?

If you have spent a few minutes surfing TV channels, you quickly come to the conclusion that much of what is out there is toxic to happiness. Spend 10 minutes watching *Jersey Shore* or *Housewives of Beverly Hills* and you see very unhappy people dealing with their "problems" in very unproductive ways.

There is another part of honoring oneself that goes considerably deeper. It has to do with nurturing the soul. It means coming to fully know and appreciate who we are. And it is achieved by probing deep inside ourselves to determine what we are passionate about and believe. What values and principles do we hold dear? What and who do we love? What are our strengths and weaknesses, our dreams? What do we wish to honor, and what legacy do we wish to leave?

Taking time to consider these deeper questions — to honor our souls — helps us become centered, to face adversity, to deal with change and to find greater happiness.

Finally, a key part of honoring our minds, bodies and spirit is exercise. There are hundreds of studies on the benefits of exercise and they all point to the same conclusion: It is important to our health, our longevity and our happiness. Exercise is preventative and curative in regards to heart disease, stroke, hypertension, diabetes, obesity, even some forms of cancer. Exercise is also essential to keeping our brains healthy. John Median, author of *Brain Rules,* concludes that aerobic exercise "slashes your lifetime risk of Alzheimer's in half and your risk of general dementia by 60 percent."

Yet our society is more sedentary than ever, with some very adverse consequences. If you don't exercise, start. It doesn't have to be vigorous. Do what is appropriate for your body. Start with a brief walk. The benefits accrue from less than a half hour three or four times a week. But as you make it part of your routine, my guess is you will find you miss it the other days and begin to do it daily. I walk three to four miles almost every morning. I had to have my hips replaced about 10 years ago and now I find walking an incredible joy. I think it helps me keep my weight down, but perhaps more importantly it is a time of reflection . . . a time to honor not just my body, but my mind and soul. The simple advice for happiness is keep moving.

Being Altruistic & Practicing Acts of Kindness

Altruism has been called the great paradox. When you give something to someone else, you're the one who feels best. Giving is getting. Studies show that happy people are altruistic, and that altruistic people are happy.
—Dan Baker, *What Happy People Know*

There is a high degree of correlation between altruism and happiness. They correlate for good reason. In Dan Baker's *What Happy People Know*, he identifies two major fears that afflict most of us through much of our lives: "I won't **be** enough" and "I won't **have** enough." People who can be altruistic have overcome the fear of not having enough and, therefore, can be generous with their resources. Positive psychologists also will tell you that, just as with ice cream or a massage, being altruistic actually lights up the pleasure centers of the brain.

Before my illness, one characteristic I felt least good about was an inability to be generous with my assets. We made contributions to various causes, but still I felt that I was stingy. That changed with my illness and a little encouragement from Phyllis.

About three months after my diagnosis of leukemia, we decided to attend a reception sponsored by the Leukemia & Lymphoma Society (LLS). Dr. John Byrd was the featured speaker. John is one of the leading research scientists at the James Cancer Center working to find better ways to manage my type of blood cancer.

Before heading out that evening, Phyllis suggested we make a donation to the LLS while we were there. As we headed out the door, I grabbed the checkbook. We have always had a simple way of figuring how much money to give to a cause. We each express a number, and if they are different we talk it out until we reach a consensus.

On our way to the event, we started our negotiation. Phyllis suggested that since I have the illness, I should go first.

I thought about it for a minute or two and said: "I think that supporting this research could possibly make a difference in finding better ways to manage this illness, if not for me, maybe for others, so I am thinking really big, like maybe $5,000. What do you think?"

Without hesitation, she said, "I think we should find a way to give $1 million." Tell me again who has the illness? I almost drove off the road.

As I regained composure, I started to list all the reasons we couldn't possibly give that much money. My answer had no effect on her. So I tried another argument, "Let's put a million dollars in our will, if we have that much left."

To which she responded: "Let me see if I understand what you are saying. You want us to wait until we have passed away and then leave a million dollars, when that money could be helping you and so many others live *now*?"

Well, we agreed to give $5,000 that night (I often win . . . in the short term). But over the next few months I came to see things Phyllis's way. This is not unusual.

I had told very few people other than my family about my illness. I decided I would take a different approach and sent an email to 90 of our closest friends, telling them I had the illness and suggesting that for every dollar they gave, we would give five. They all knew how cheap I was, so many thought this was a good way to cause me a little pain.

At the bottom of the email, I wrote, "Please pass it on to anyone who might be interested" — this cost us dearly. With the help of family, relatives and hundreds of friends, the email had generated close to $1.5 million at last count. Our gratitude runs deep for our generous family members and friends.

There are several medications in trial to treat my form of blood cancer, including a promising new drug, Ibrutinib, which is being tested at the James Cancer Center 3 miles from where I live. This trial drug is showing remarkable ability to limit the growth of the cancer with a minimum of side effects. As I write this, the Food and Drug Administration has just granted "breakthrough" status to Ibrutinib, thus enabling it to move more quickly to the marketplace. Such work would not be possible without the generous support of the LLS and thousands of generous donors, including those that responded to our email. Thank you.

It took a life-threatening illness for me to learn the value of altruism, but it doesn't have to be that way. Giving our assets and our skills to something we care about does lead to happiness. Living in fear of not having enough is a lousy way to live. Many of us don't have sufficient resources to make large charitable contributions to causes we hold dear. But giving generously of the resources we do have — time, passion, commitment or money — is a sure pathway to greater happiness.

Thinking with Abundance

> *God make me thin, but if you can't, make all my girlfriends fat.*
>
> —Anonymous

OK, here is a test for you. Your best friend just got something you really want — a new BMW, a new house, a promotion, a baby, a big salary increase, tenure. Think of something you really want and your friend has just gotten it. When you learn that your friend has gotten this you say, "I am so happy for you; that is great!" But here is the test question: How do you really feel?

If you are like many of us, you aren't really all that happy. In fact, you are a little jealous and angry that you didn't get it. To the degree you feel that way, you are suffering from scarcity thinking — a perspective that robs many of us from feeling happy.

I know scarcity thinking well. There is an antidote for it: thinking with abundance. But abundance thinking is something that I struggle with daily. My guess is many of you, particularly those of you who are highly competitive, find this a struggle as well.

Scarcity thinking is when you think most of life is win or lose. If someone wins, then by definition — your definition anyway — someone must lose. In other words, we see the world as a pie, and if someone else gets a piece of the pie, then there has to be that much less for everyone else. On the other hand, abundance thinking is when we see the world as limitless and one person's gain does not have to be another's loss.

The first year I taught a winter term class at DePauw, one of my students was a young woman who was a senior studying pre-med. She had applied to a program at the Mayo Clinic, to which only about 35 students were accepted nationwide. During the winter term she was waiting anxiously to hear if she had been accepted. By coincidence, another student with whom she was good friends had also applied. One day she came into class and was ebullient. She smiled radiantly as she told me her friend had been accepted to the program. When I asked if she had heard yet, she answered that no she hadn't, but she was still hopeful she would be accepted.

As she walked away, I wondered how I would respond in a similar situation. Could I have found it within myself to feel joy for someone else, when I didn't know my own fate? She was practicing abundant thinking, and doing so is a key skill to happiness.

I struggle with this skill perhaps more than any of the other happiness skills I have shared in this book. I think I understand why. Many years ago I took part in a *Life Styles Inventory* test. I filled out this fairly detailed questionnaire intended to determine my predominant behavioral styles. The *Life Styles Inventory* comprises 12 styles, such as self-actualizing, affiliative, power, achievement, competitive and oppositional.

When I met with the psychologist who administered the evaluation, he said, "Doug, I have been doing this for nearly 30 years and I have never had anyone as high as you on the style of 'self-actualizing' — loving to learn and to improve oneself."

I was thinking (since I judge everything that comes before me), "This is good!"

He then said, "I have also never had anyone as high on 'competitiveness.' In fact, with those two styles there is almost no room for other styles."

Still thinking the feedback was great, I said, "Well, I was a bit of an athlete in college and winning has always been important to me. . . ." He interrupted me and said, "Doug, I want you to know that 'competitive' is **NOT** a positive trait."

What?

"Wait a minute!" I said. "It has to be a positive trait! Competition and winning are what it is all about. I would have never had the success I have had if I wasn't competitive."

He rolled his eyes, then took a deep breath; he had obviously had this conversation before. Passing a piece of paper over to me he let me read the description of "competitive":

> *The competitive scale measures our need to establish a sense of self-worth through competing against and comparing ourselves to others. While it is largely encouraged and accepted as a measure of success, competitive behavior is not an effective predictor of achievement in business, sports, or life in general. In fact, studies have shown that people who come out ahead in competitive situations focus on performance excellence, or the process of doing well, rather than on the end result of winning.*
>
> *Competitive people compete to overcome doubts about themselves and their abilities. Competitors attach their sense of self-worth so securely to winning and being seen as the best that they set up "all or nothing" situations for themselves.*
>
> *In general, the competitive style is characterized by:*
> - *The association of self-worth with winning and losing*
> - *A need for recognition and praise from others*
> - *A tendency toward aggressiveness*
> - *Reckless, hip-shooting behavior and unnecessary risk-taking*
> - *A "win-lose" orientation that distorts perspective and goals*
> - *An extreme fear of failure.*
>   —Life Styles Inventory, Human Synergistics
>   International, *Self-Development Guide*

As I read this I realized it described me perfectly — particularly the "reckless, hip shooting behavior." I recalled the shortcut by Big Moose Lake that long-ago January day. Gulp

That conversation with the psychologist occurred about 15 years ago, but it has probably been only in the last few years that I have come to understand how right he was.

For those of us who are driven, instead of inspired, to succeed — "alpha males," if you will — the concept that being highly competitive is not a positive trait is more than a little difficult to grasp. We tend to think that competitiveness is the very foundation of what enables us to be successful. Without it we think we would just sit around and wait for something to happen.

Competition can be a driver of behavior, and it can result in progress and achievement. But I believe there is a deeper level of motivation that results in greater progress, greater success and greater well-being. It is cooperation. If we focus more on cooperation than competition, if we can find win-win situations, versus the win-lose, we will be happier and in the end, even more successful.

In business, leaders can either focus on beating the competition, or they can focus on creating an organization that serves its customers with superior products and services, enables its employees to grow and prosper, brings attractive returns to its owners, helps its suppliers thrive, and enhances the communities where it operates. The second scenario is more about cooperation than it is about competition. Competition is great on the tennis court or on the golf course, but we would do well not to carry it into the workplace.

I believe if we are inspired by win-win and cooperation, versus win-lose and competition, we will find greater success in the marketplace than those who are focused on beating others. As Alfie Kohn asks in *No Contest: The Case Against Competition:* "How can we do our best when we are spending our energies trying to make others lose — and fearing they will make us lose?"

I also think we will be happier. Sonja Lyubomirsky, a psychology professor at University of California, Riverside, and author of *The How of Happiness,* said that when she asked those who were less happy whom they competed against, they went on and on. When she asked the happiest the same question, they hardly knew what she was talking about.

Competition serves a purpose, but it is a means, not an end. When we make it the goal, we take our eye off the actions that really lead to success and happiness. Winning isn't everything and winning isn't the only thing. It is only a part of what makes up success. Organizations and people that work to find win-win solutions and focus more on cooperation than competition, I believe, find greater joy in what they do and greater success in the marketplace.

Competition is about comparison, and as one of my students was fond of saying, "Comparison is the thief of joy."

Mastering Our Stories

Among all the things we don't control, we do have control over our stories. Individual responsibility is contained in the act of selecting and constantly revising the master narrative we tell about ourselves. The most important power we have is the power to help select the lens through which we see reality.

—David Brooks

You and I have a companion. It is a companion that never leaves us. It is there as soon as we wake up and it is with us throughout the day. When we go to bed, it is still there. It may well keep us awake for hours. That companion is our "mental chatter" or our "inner voice."

If you think about it, there is a monologue going on in your head every waking moment. Your inner voice makes judgments about you and others and about most everything that happens — and it is almost always negative. It is negative because it is a voice of fear.

Before I started studying and teaching happiness, I didn't realize how negative this voice was. In fact, I didn't even realize I had this voice until I read Srikumar Raos' *Are You Ready to Succeed?* I decided I would spend 24 hours listening to and observing my inner voice. What I discovered was my inner voice was ugly, really ugly. It shouted all kinds of derogatory thoughts about me and everyone else for almost the entire day. It said things about me I would never let someone else say, and it said things about others I would never openly express. It sat in judgment of everyone and everything.

As I have studied this further, I realize that not all of us have this voice. There are a few people who have a much more encouraging voice that thinks kind thoughts about others and themselves. There's an even smaller number of people who don't have an inner voice talking to them at all. They experience the world without this inner voice. But I have also found the majority of people seem to have a negative, judging inner voice. As the song by Alabama goes, we really do have a "jukebox in the corner of [our] minds," but, for most of us, it is playing an ugly song. We are better than this voice and we have the option of rising above it.

Our emotions don't just happen. And this inner voice doesn't just happen, we create it. And if we create it, we can change it. Put simply, we can either master this inner voice or we can be mastered by it. If we master this voice, we will experience far greater happiness. But doing so is not easy.

Most of us think our feelings and actions are caused by events.

Someone cuts us off as we drive to work and we feel angry and act aggressively. We think it is the event that caused us to feel and act that way.

In truth, between the event and how we feel and act, we tell a story. We tell a story that explains what we see. We **always** tell a story.

The story is our minds' attempt to put context and meaning around events. What we respond to is not the event as much as the story we tell ourselves. In the event of the person who cuts us off in traffic, we tell ourselves a story about what a jerk the driver is and how inconsiderate he is. Our feelings would be very different if we thought that he was in the midst of a medical emergency trying to get to the hospital. Likewise when a student comes into my class late, my response will be generated more by the story I tell myself about the event than the event itself. This happens hundreds of times a day. Our feelings and actions are based on the stories we tell, and often the stories are neither accurate nor conducive to happiness.

Herein lies the problem and the opportunity. We can change how we feel and how we respond by changing the story. We can think about the little voice going on inside our head and begin to be masters of it.

I have been working on mastering my inner voice for several years now. Whereas the inner voice used to shout at me and abuse me terribly, it is much quieter today. It never fully goes away and it still says some pretty negative stuff, but it is quieter, almost tentative. I have also learned to recognize it for what it is. It is my voice of fear, and I suppose it thinks its job is to protect me and motivate me. I have found better ways to look out for myself and inspire myself than listening to this voice of fear. I am trying to become the master of this voice.

Jill Bolte was a brain researcher at Harvard University until she suffered a stroke. After recovering, she wrote *Stroke of Insight*, in which she considers her inner voice:

> *Many of us spend an inordinate amount of time and energy degrading, insulting and criticizing ourselves and others for having made a 'wrong' decision. When you berate yourself, have you ever questioned: who inside you is doing the yelling and at whom are you yelling? Have you ever noticed how these negative internal thought patterns have a tendency to generate increased levels of inner hostility and/ or raised levels of anxiety . . . and eventually [affect] how you treat others and, thus, what you attract.*
> —Jill Bolte, *Stroke of Insight*

Jim Loehr in *The Power of Story* considers the personal story: "Often we don't need new facts, we need new stories . . . change your stories and you change your life."

Psychologists call this changing of our stories "redirecting" or "story editing." Most of our stories need a lot of editing. We can change our stories from fear to love and in so doing significantly increase our happiness.

The ability to master our inner voice is a key to happiness. Perhaps the most important conversations we have are the ones we have with ourselves. What stories do you tell yourself? What tone does the voice inside your head take? Is it supportive, or does it tear you and most everyone else down?

Some stories we tell ourselves once or twice, and they really make very little difference in our lives. Others we tell ourselves repeatedly over the course of our lifetimes and they shape our entire lives.

For years I told myself: "I am not good at remembering names." As long as I told myself that story, I wasn't good with names. The day I stopped telling myself this story and spent a couple of hours working on techniques to remember names, I suddenly was pretty good at it. Now forgetting names is probably not all that damaging, but consider these two stories and how they shape the lives of those that tell them. Story one: "I am an alcoholic. Both of my parents were alcoholics, what do you expect?" Story two: "I don't drink. Both of my parents were alcoholics, what do you expect?"

What stories do you tell yourself that shape your life? Do you need to edit some of your stories? Which ones prevent you from finding happiness?

Finding Meaning, Purpose & Flow

A mountain climber may be close to freezing, utterly exhausted, in danger of falling into a bottomless crevasse, yet he wouldn't want to be anywhere else. Sipping a cocktail under a palm tree at the edge of the turquoise ocean is nice, but it just may not compare to the exhilaration he feels on that freezing ridge.
        —Martin Seligman, *Authentic Happiness*

The next two skills of happiness really underlie all the others. In my opinion, happiness in the present is most dependent on these two skills: 1) becoming engaged and passionate about a meaningful purpose, and 2) forming and cherishing healthy relationships. Figure out how to do those two things — which can take a lifetime — and you will most likely be happy. Let's deal first with discovering our purpose.

For my winter term course at DePauw, students are required to read two texts. The first is *What Happy People Know* by Dan Baker. In it Dr. Baker helps people overcome situations or decisions that robbed them of happiness. It is a profound book, and I personally owe to him many of my own insights into happiness to him. The second is *Man's Search for Meaning* by Viktor Frankl. The Library of Congress called it one of the 10 most influential books of the 20th century.

Viktor Frankl was a noted psychiatrist in Germany before the start of World War II. During the war he was interned in several concentration camps, including Auschwitz. He survived. His wife, parents and other family members did not. When released from Auschwitz, he wrote his famous book in nine days. It is the story of what he learned as a prisoner. From that experience, he founded what has been called the "Third School of Viennese Psychology," or "Logotherapy."

The first two schools of Viennese Psychology were established by Sigmund Freud and Alfred Adler. First, Freud suggested that man's fundamental struggle was with pleasure. Later, Adler came along and said man's fundamental struggle was with power. But after surviving the Holocaust, Frankl insisted man's fundamental struggle was not with pleasure or power, but with meaning — finding meaning and purpose in our existence. He said that without meaning, we are lost and have little will to survive. He concluded that those who survived the concentration camps — and only one of 28 who entered did — had something deeply important they yet wanted to achieve.

Those who live with joy are invariably engaged in activities that they view as meaningful and that use their unique talents. In the last 15 years, the concept of flow has emerged to explain this phenomenon.

Flow occurs when we use our talents to meet some challenge that deeply engages us and to which we happily cede our energy and attention. We seem to lose all sense of time as we focus on the activity. One example is kids on the beach who spend hours completely absorbed in creating a sand castle. Other examples would be the rock climber described by Martin Seligman in the quote at the beginning of this section or a sports team with all players in sync and working incredibly well together.

Modified from Mihaly Csikszentmihalyi, *Flow*

Experiencing flow often brings intense joy, especially when we are doing something we think is important or meaningful. The key is finding the sweet spot between stress, where the challenge exceeds the skill, and boredom, where talent exceeds the challenge. When I lead a class at DePauw or at Canyon Ranch, I frequently experience flow. It takes every ounce of energy, focus, IQ, EQ and skill I have to meet the challenge of having a successful class. When the class is over I am exhausted, but the experience is an incredible joy.

If you've ever played a new video game, you will recognize this balance. At first you play at an easy level. As your skill increases, you move up to a more advanced level or you will become bored. Finding that balance between challenge and skill is the path to flow. Without purpose, flow is not possible.

Ever wonder why some people like to rock climb? I think it is because of flow. They are using their unique talents in meeting a challenge that is very important to them — staying alive. They are also totally in the present or "doing now what I am doing now." They cannot worry about the bills that haven't been paid or the test they have to take tomorrow.

Through teaching at DePauw, I have come to believe that significant purpose also precedes significant learning. I have observed that my students fall across a broad spectrum of interests and capabilities. In particular, they run from being what I call "ShamWows" to "ducks." Let me explain. I have certain students that are incredibly engaged in class. They take copious notes, they listen intently, and they participate in class, expressing their thoughts and opinions. I think of them as ShamWows, after the TV commercial for the ShamWow cloth that "absorbs 12 times its weight in water."

On the other end of the spectrum are the ducks. Any subject rolls off these students like water off a duck's back. They take no notes, they don't participate much in class and they seem to have little interest in what is being covered. Now in truth, some students who are ducks in one class are ShamWows in another and some days the students become one or the other. As a teacher, I work to reach all my students, but I also work to turn as many as possible into ShamWows, since ShamWows will invariably do better in school and they will be happier. Ducks have a special place in my heart, however, since for most of my college student years I was one.

I have found that what determines whether one is a ShamWow or a duck is often clarity of purpose. Those students who have something they want to achieve are far more likely to be engaged in the class. Their purpose gives meaning and context to the subjects we discuss in class. I used to think that this meant they had a clear vision about what they wanted to do once they graduated, such as be a doctor, lawyer or teacher. I have come to realize that often this isn't the case. When I asked one student, who was clearly a ShamWow, what he wanted to do when he graduated, he said he had no idea. When I asked him what he wanted to major in, he was equally unsure.

But then he said something that really intrigued me. He said: "I just want to get as much out of this college experience as I can. College to me is like a smorgasbord of opportunities to learn all sorts of things. I want to get as much out of college as I can academically, athletically and socially." Wow! I couldn't conceive of a better purpose for a young college student. His purpose served him very well.

I suggest to my students that purpose is like underwear: Don't be caught without it! So they won't be caught without it, as part of my winter term class, students work on clarifying a mission for themselves. In helping them discover their missions, I modify Frederick Buechner's quote to read: ". . . the place where your deep gladness, [your deep understanding] and the world's deep hunger meet."

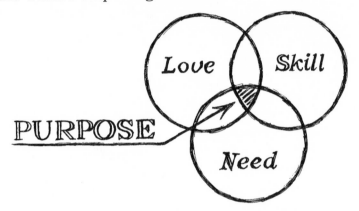

I believe that where these three circles come together is where our purpose is to be found. It's the intersection of what we love to do (gladness), what we are particularly skilled at (understanding) and where the world has a need (hunger).

For those of us well beyond the college experience, the challenge regarding "purpose" may be very different than that of my students. Many of us are actively engaged in a career or some activity that occupies far more of our time than we would like. For many of us the challenge then becomes making sure that in pursuing careers or interests, we don't neglect other things that are important to us. As I look back on my life, I feel that in the pursuit of my career objectives I often neglected my obligations to my family, my community and myself. I think I was too narrow in my focus, which negatively affected my family life and my health.

Before my illness, I found myself chasing an increasingly narrow and confining objective — a finish line that didn't really exist. My work took on an increasingly big portion of my life and how I defined myself. My life became increasingly one-dimensional, and I think my health, my family and, surprisingly, my work suffered because of it. The trick is to integrate every aspect of our lives, so that what we learn and do in one aspect of our lives benefits every other aspect of our lives.

The act of creating a personal mission statement has served me well these past few years. When I am true to this mission, my joy increases. And when I vary from it, I always end up paying a price. I will share my current mission statement with you, not to have you use it as a template, but to stimulate your own thinking about what is important to you and what you would like to achieve. I would encourage you to read it, but to set it aside as you develop your own mission statement. You don't want a "suit off the rack." It is important that your mission statement is unique and reflects you.

My mission was relatively easy to write, living it is considerably more difficult.

DOUGLAS A. SMITH — MISSION

My power, my wisdom, my uniqueness, my life is fulfilled by acting in a manner consistent with this mission.

In a world of scarcity, I will act with abundance. In a world of fear, I will act with love. In a world of anger and retribution, I will act with forgiveness. In a world that is fragmented, I will integrate all aspects of my life. In a world of materialism, I will be guided by my spirit and a concern for what is enduring.

I will grow. I will learn to listen before speaking. I will learn patience. I will increasingly overcome my selfish desires. I will not let the pettiness and the frustration or challenges of the moment mask the significance and the beauty of the gifts and the life I have been given. I will remain appreciative and grateful. I will develop and utilize my talents for the enhancement of this world.

I will serve my family, *for it is through them that I create the greatest value. I will remain faithful to the vows I made to my wife over 40 years ago by consistently "loving, honoring, cherishing and serving" her. My wife and I will create a home that is constant and abundant in its love and security, and that is therefore conducive to each of us leading successful, meaningful and fulfilling lives. As the primary wage earner, I will provide financial well-being to enable our family to function. Finally, I will remain a friend and support to my extended family and all those with whom I come in contact.*

I will serve my vocation, *for it is through work that I develop and direct many of my talents. My work is to understand what leads to a meaningful, flourishing life, to live consistent with this understanding, and to help others do the same. As a winter term faculty member at DePauw I will enhance the lives of the students I serve by sharing my knowledge and experience concerning happiness — what is happiness, what leads to it and what does not lead to it — in an effort to help them increasingly live considered, consequential and fulfilling lives. As a leader of classes at Canyon Ranch and elsewhere my work will be centered on enabling people to live more fulfilling, loving lives. I will serve as an effective and trusted advisor to various CEOs and leaders of corporations and not-for-profit organizations, helping them create abundant organizations by clarifying their visions and increasingly engaging their stakeholders in the pursuit of that vision. Finally, I will place my message in a book so that I can reach an ever-larger audience.*

I will serve the communities *within which I live and work, for it is through this service that I am able to give back a portion of what I have received. I will give 10 percent of our income* *and an increasingly larger percentage of my time to causes that enhance our world communities, with particular focus on health, education and the environment.*

I will serve the substantive needs of self, for I can only achieve this mission by caring for and nurturing myself. I do this daily by being physically active, eating well, nourishing my soul through reflection and worship, and expanding my mind and vision through continuous learning.

By fulfilling this mission I find meaning and value in life, the world finds meaning and value in me, and I find joy in this journey.

When I look back on this mission statement, I notice there is nothing about competition in it. It doesn't measure my contribution or work or efforts versus someone else. It simply states what I wish to achieve, and if I do fulfill this mission, it is win/win for everyone concerned. I also notice that I can't fulfill the mission by throwing my family, my community or my own personal well-being "under the bus" in order to achieve my work goals. Instead it challenges me to find ways to integrate all aspects of my life.

For those who are nearing retirement age, the challenge is probably the transition of purpose. I suppose it is possible to find joy in stopping work and playing golf most every day. But for some, this isn't enough. I know that without being engaged in something that uses my talents (and playing golf is not one of my talents), it is difficult for me to experience a deep sense of joy. In fact, my mind tends to gravitate toward depression. I like to play golf, but I love to teach, to mentor, to consult, to gain new insights, particularly about leadership and happiness. To share those insights with others and to learn from others brings me tremendous joy. Figuring out new ways to use talents we have developed during our careers, or developing new talents and finding ways to utilize them, is an important transition for many of us as our careers wind down. James Hollis's *Finding Meaning in the Second Half of Life* is an excellent resource for those approaching such a transition.

I think it is difficult to be happy without purpose. I believe Viktor Frankl's conclusion was right: We all search for meaning in life. In large part we find this meaning by passionately pursuing some purpose or purposes we deem of value.

The other way we find meaning is through relationships. Let us turn to relationships as a final skill to finding happiness in the present.

Cherishing Relationships

Relationships are the key to happiness. Happiness is Love: Full Stop.
—George E. Vaillant, M.D.

Many of you may have seen the movie *Cast Away*. The plot revolves around a FedEx employee, Chuck Noland, played by Tom Hanks, who is the only survivor of a plane crash in the South Pacific. He finds himself marooned on an uninhabited island where he lives for the next five years. The movie has two crucial props that symbolize purpose and relationships, the last two skills of finding happiness in the present.

During Noland's first few days on the island, a number of FedEx packages wash up on the beach. Noland proceeds to open them. One package contains a ballet tutu that he converts into a fishing net. Others contain a pair of ice skates, which he turns into an ax, and a videotape, which he uses to lash together logs to make a raft. When Noland gets to the last unopened package, he hesitates. He doesn't open this package. Instead, he sets it aside. When he finally attempts to leave the island and find his way back to civilization, Noland takes the unopened package with him.

I believe the package represents "purpose." A career FedEx employee, Noland felt compelled to deliver the package. And for those of you who remember the movie, he does eventually deliver the package and it seems to be the start of a new chapter in his life.

There is a second prop in *Cast Away* that is perhaps even more easily recognized as a symbol: Wilson. One of the packages that washes up on the beach contains a soccer ball. After several weeks on the island, Noland draws a face on the ball and then places sticks in the top of the ball for hair. Wilson, the ball's brand name, becomes his constant companion. Noland shares his thoughts, frustrations, ideas, longings, hopes and fears with Wilson.

When Noland leaves the island, he takes Wilson and the unopened FedEx box with him on the raft. After several weeks at sea, one day he wakes to find Wilson floating away. He uses a tether of videotape to swim to Wilson, who is just beyond his reach. At this point, he must decide to swim after Wilson and release the tether or stay with the raft to avoid drowning. He reluctantly decides to return to the raft. He is devastated. In fact, he gives up his pursuit of finding rescue.

I believe Wilson represents the importance of relationships to survival. In order to survive his five years alone on the island, Noland created a relationship with a soccer ball to minimize his isolation.

Relationships have been a key to survival throughout human history. We often talk about survival of the fittest, but when you think about it we are not a very impressive physical species. We don't have sharp claws or teeth, we aren't particularly strong, and we can't run as fast as most of our predators. Individually, we make a pretty good target or meal. It is collectively that we are powerful. What enabled humans to survive hundreds of thousands of years ago was the ability to come together, to cooperate, to be in relationship. Bound together, we suddenly had the strength to protect ourselves and become the hunters, versus the hunted.

Forming and maintaining healthy, positive relationships leads to greater happiness. I have three suggestions for improving your relationship-building skills. The first is simple to grasp, but hard to execute.

Many of us make a very common and often devastating mistake. We trade relationships for other goals. This is particularly true as we take on more responsibility at work.

I definitely was guilty of this, and I think I know why many of us make this trade off. At work, we often have very tangible, measureable goals. Being goal driven, we gravitate to those tasks we can measure, check off on our to-do lists and be rewarded for. Relationships are different. They are less measureable, less concrete and, while important, they would seem to take care of themselves — until they don't.

As I rose in my career, I made less time for relationships and more time for work. It was not a healthy trade off.

So the first way to improve your relationships is simple, but very hard to execute: Make time for them. Canadians have a wonderful phrase for expressing that they like someone. They say, "I have a lot of time for them." It is an accurate description for what we do with folks we really care about. Make time for your spouse, partner, children, family and friends, and when you do, give them all 140 bits of information capability as discussed earlier in this chapter. Relationships should be a priority in our lives, not something we trade off each time work gets challenging.

The second way to improve relationships is to raise your jen ratio. The jen ratio is a very simple measure. It is your number of positive interactions to negative interactions. You can measure it anywhere — on a playground, in school, at work or at home. It can be a measure of the positive versus negative interactions you have with your friends, your spouse or significant other, your kids, your entire family.

Let's start by considering the jen ratio within a relationship. There is actually a specific name for this ratio in a marriage — the Gottman Ratio, after John and Julie Gottman. For a good marriage the ratio should be at least 5:1. That is five positive interactions for each negative interaction. For a few days observe the interactions you have with your spouse and consider which are negative and which are positive. Make it a game. Then figure out how you might increase the positive interactions and reduce the negatives ones.

At work the jen ratio is often called the Losada ratio. Interestingly, for work the most effective organizations have a ratio of at least 3:1 and not more than 12:1. My assumption is that above 12:1 genuine, necessary conflict is not occurring.

The third and probably most powerful way to improve your overall skill of relationships is to improve your EQ, or emotional intelligence. Most people have heard of EQ for good reason — it's important both to success in life and to happiness.

Many people believe that EQ is more important than IQ for professional success. As Daniel Goleman writes in *Emotional Intelligence*:

> *Psychologists agree that IQ contributes only about 20 percent of the factors that determine success. A full 80 percent comes from other factors, including what I call emotional intelligence.*

Clearly, if we are talking about brain surgery or rocket science (or, as George Bush would say, "rocket surgery") then IQ plays a critical role. But for most occupations — and for being happy — EQ plays a more important role. Warren Buffett famously said, "If you have a 140 IQ, sell 25 points. You don't need them."

EQ is really four separate skills that, when practiced together, lead to an ability to have enduring, productive relationships with others. The first skill is being aware of what we are feeling. It is the ability to step back from ourselves and consider how we feel and why we feel that way. It is the ability to understand our feelings. People of high EQ are aware of what they feel and can pinpoint why they feel a particular way.

The second skill is the ability to manage how we respond to our feelings. When we are angry, it may or may not be productive to express that anger. If we choose to express our anger, how we express it is equally important. People with high EQ are aware of what they are feeling and are able to manage how they respond to those feelings so that they find productive ways to express themselves.

The third skill of EQ is the ability to sense what others are feeling and to empathize with them. In effect, it is the ability to "know where people are coming from."

The final skill is the ability to pull all of the prior skills together such that we use our awareness of our own emotions, the management of those emotions and the awareness of other's emotions to create conditions for effective interactions.

EQ, unlike IQ, is changeable. We can improve upon these skills. *The Emotional Intelligence Quick Book* by Travis Bradberry and Jean Greaves is an excellent resource for working to improve one's EQ and in so doing form more enduring, healthy relationships.

There's another key to effective relationships: Don't break important commitments you make to others. Relationships often take years to develop, but can be quickly destroyed when we break the trust upon which they have been built.

Integrating purpose and relationships effectively has always been a struggle for me. I repeatedly traded off relationships for purpose, spending way too many hours working and, when I was at home, being often distracted by thoughts about the office.

One night, when our son Greg was 8 years old and I had been working many long hours, we were at the dinner table and Greg said, "Dad, I think we need a suggestion box." I said, "OK." When I came home the next night, I found in the entrance hall a decorated shoebox sporting the phrase "Suggestion Box" in block letters. As we sat down for dinner, Greg said, "Dad, I think there is a suggestion in the suggestion box." So I went into the hallway and opened the box to find a little yellow sticky note with Greg's name on the back. It has been on my mirror now for 26 years. It reminds me what is really important (see next page).

Could there be a clearer, more powerful message to not repeatedly trade off relationships for purpose? Yet I did for years after receiving this note. I wish I had a simple solution for successfully integrating purpose and relationships — the two loadstars of happiness. Some of the ideas in this book will hopefully help, especially in creating a mission statement to define what is of value to you.

I WiSh
Dad had
more Time
To play

I think with time I have gotten better at integrating purpose and relationships. The key has been defining my foundational principles and then making my behavior increasingly consistent with those principles no matter where I am. Mahatma Gandhi said, "Happiness is when what you think, what you say and what you do are in harmony." Striving to do this helps me make more win-win decisions for all concerned.

Chapter 9

ALL THE WAYS
I WENT ASTRAY

*People will always choose what makes them
happy, once they have exhausted all the other
possibilities.*
       —Author, with apologies to Winston Churchill

While happiness is the ultimate goal in our decision making,
we still can make choices that bring us misery. I am no
exception.

Looking back on my life, I realize there are a series of dead-
end paths I headed down in my pursuit of happiness. I have
organized these into five groups. My guess is you will be
familiar with most, if not all, of them.

All five dead ends are similar and devious in their allure in
that at first they seem a shortcut to happiness. As we travel
them further, however, they invariably disappoint — and are
often difficult to get out of. They ensnare us, even though
we recognize they do not bring us joy. They are, as Carrie
Underwood's song *Cowboy Casanova* suggests, "candy-
coated misery."

The Pleasure Dead End

This dead end has been around for all of human existence. The Roman philosopher Seneca 2,000 years ago said, "So-called pleasures when they go beyond a certain limit are but punishments." I think he was correct. Pleasure is a dead end that snares most of us at one point or another. Pleasure is a wonderful part of happiness, but only a part, and a fleeting part at that.

You and I are experts in pleasure because our minds are wired for pleasure. Our minds are much attuned to what feels good, and they store away in memory exactly how and when we experienced pleasure, so we can receive it again.

But there is a dark side to pleasure, and falling into that dark side is pretty easy. We experience the dark side when we try to make pleasure the core of our happiness or an enduring source of happiness. Pleasure has some peculiar properties that lead to disappointment, and often unhappiness, when we place it at the center of our pursuit of happiness

Here is what we know about pleasure:

- It feels good. When we do something that brings us pleasure, it actually lights up certain parts of our brain known as the pleasure center. Pleasure chemically alters our mood by raising the levels of certain neurotransmitters in our brains, especially one called serotonin.
- It depends on an external stimulus. Pleasure happens because some stimulus has been added or taken away.
- It is the *change* in stimulus that gives pleasure.

And here is where the trouble begins:

- We adapt to it; through two processes known as "habituation" and "adaptation." Once we are used to

the stimulus, it no longer has the capability to bring us pleasure — unless we add more of the stimulus.
* It can be chemically replicated.

Many of the things that bring us pleasure are pretty hard to abuse. But certain things that bring us "pleasure" have a lot of potential for abuse: sex, alcohol, drugs, and gambling, to name a few. Marriages, families, relationships, health, lives are destroyed by these forms of pleasure when they become the focal point of people's lives.

Kenny Chesney's song *Demons* captures it well:

> *"There's things that I can't leave alone,*
> *'Cause they won't leave me alone.*
> *What I want ain't what I need,*
> *Still I reach for the things I crave.*
> *Then try to run away.*
> *Am I afraid of being free? You tell me.*
> *'Cause when I'm not chasing demons,*
> *There's demons chasing me."*

Pleasure can be a wonderful part of our lives and a source of happiness, but it can also be an incredible source of sadness. Alcoholics, drug addicts and sex addicts are not happy people. Instead, they are caught in the grips of something that controls their lives and brings more misery than happiness to themselves and often to others.

The Money Dead End

Money definitely has an effect on happiness. It can bring us joy or it can be a dead end in our pursuit of happiness. The relationship between money and happiness is complex. The answer to the question "Does money buy happiness?" is not as easy as "yes" or "no." But there is an answer to that question, and those that figure out the answer, particularly those that do so early in life, have a considerably greater chance of being happy. The answer depends on how much money, how the money is used and how the money is obtained.

Let's start with the question: How much? There is definitely a positive correlation between income and happiness. Meaning that as income goes up so does our level of happiness. This is particularly true at the lower income levels. It seems that in general poverty is not fun, or as Sophie Tucker says, "I've been rich and I've been poor. Rich is better."

Not being able to provide for ourselves or our families does not make for happy living conditions. In the United States this relationship between income and happiness holds pretty strongly, until you reach a household income of about $60,000. After that, the relationship weakens considerably, meaning that more income does not necessarily bring more happiness.

For many of us, the idea that a lot more money will make us much happier is spurious, but oh so hard to let go. Materialism and social comparison run very deep in our wiring. They are an instinctive part of our biological make up. For more than 90 percent of our existence as a species we have been hunters and gatherers. In such a society those individuals who were best at obtaining and hording scarce resources dominated. That instinct has morphed into materialism nowadays, with many of us obsessed with possessions. But materialism and happiness are actually inversely correlated. Materialism is toxic to happiness. The more room we make in our lives for material possessions, the less space we have for people and relationships. Studies show those who score highest on materialism are among the least happy.

It is easy for us to mistake the momentary elation we get from purchasing or obtaining material possessions for happiness. If we seek to find personal satisfaction and other nonmaterial qualities through material possessions, we will be disappointed for they simply cannot provide this. People sometimes quote the Bible, saying, "Money is the root of all evil." To be accurate, the quote is, "The LOVE of money is the root of all evil."

This leads me to the question: How is the money used? Since poverty is not fun, we need to invest first in ourselves and our families, meaning our money should be directed first toward shelter, clothing, food, education, retirement and, then, leisure. To do this requires both making an income and saving some of it. It requires that we view money as a valuable resource and treat it as such. A University of Michigan study suggests that 70 percent of American households have saved less than $10,000. The average credit card holder has nearly that much in credit card debt. Earning, saving and investing money for the future is an important part of achieving happiness. Figuring out how to do it smartly can be difficult, but is essential.

The lack of savings and large credit card debt, as indicated in the Michigan study, may in part reflect the materialistic bent of our society. Surveys always show that "money" is one of the three items that couples fight about most often — the other two are "relatives" and "sex." Using our money wisely to provide for ourselves and our families is conducive to happiness. So is using our money to benefit others, particularly those who are less fortunate.

In the last chapter, we talked about altruism and its effect on happiness. Positive psychologists have conducted studies where they give participants $20. They tell half of the participants to buy something of their choosing for themselves. The other half are told to buy something of their choosing for someone they care about. When researchers subsequently measure the participants' happiness, the members of the altruistic group invariably are found to be happier.

A brief article by Margaret Coker in the *Wall Street Journal* a few years ago titled "Read My License Plate: It Cost Me a Fortune," revealed that Abdullah Al-Mannaei of the United Arab Emirates paid $14 million for a vanity license plate that displayed the number "1." His cousin spent $9 million for number "5." (I wonder if those payments were good for only one year?) When you consider that prestige and status have little to do with happiness, but altruism, gratitude and generosity have a lot to do with happiness, this investment in vanity plates probably had little return in terms of happiness. For that $23 million, one could build a school for the blind, send thousands of "Make a Wish" kids to Disney World or provide $10,000 scholarships to 2,300 kids, all of which would likely have led to much more happiness, for both the givers and the receivers.

Finally, how money is obtained plays into happiness. It seems that "earned" money brings more happiness than "unearned" money. Lottery winners and those who receive large inheritances don't seem to get much of a boost in their happiness from their cash infusions.

Lottery winners are among the favorite subjects for positive psychology studies. Most studies suggest lottery winners are often less happy six months after winning than they were before they won. Lottery winners often give up their work, buy a lot of useless stuff, destroy existing relationships, form new ill-conceived relationships and even begin a pattern of substance abuse. Maybe the lottery ticket that doesn't win is a better investment than the winning ticket, when it comes to happiness. Perhaps it is best when, as the classic commercial for Smith Barney with John Houseman stated, "We make money the old fashioned way: We earn it."

When I teach at DePauw, I try to help the students understand that money is an incredibly valuable resource and should be treated as such. Work provides both income and meaning. I think it is important for them to save a minimum of 10 percent of what they make, to do this early in their careers and to invest it wisely. I suggest they take out a loan for only three needs: an education, a house and (if they can't get to work without it) a car. They should not have any other debt. Under no circumstances should they have a loan balance on their credit card.

While money can be a dead end, perhaps money can buy happiness — you just have to know how to obtain it, save it, spend it and give it away.

The Sympathy Dead End

Strange as it seems, many of us seek happiness in sympathy. We look for others to raise us up by expressing how terrible our plight is. We are tempted to head down this dead end because we become the center of attention and we relieve ourselves of the responsibility to do something about our predicament. We make ourselves victims. Sorrow is a natural and important stage in the process of dealing with loss. Cleaving to sorrow is not. We can visit "Pity City," we just can't move there.

Interestingly, sympathy is just one of the negative emotions we can cleave to in our search for happiness. Often we hang on to anger, jealousy, envy and fear. Each of these emotions serves a purpose, but when we make them a part of our persona, they sour our relationships with others and lead to unhappiness. Psychologists often refer to this hanging on to negative emotions or stories as "story fondling."

One of the cruelest parts of the sympathy dead end is that by harboring these negative emotions, we tend to distance ourselves from the very people who can console us in difficult times. As Dan Baker states in *What Happy People Know*, "Misery may like company, but company does not like misery."

The Now Dead End

This may be the most common dead end of all. Most of us are suckers for what we want NOW. Few of us consciously ask ourselves, "Will this decision/action make me happier in the long run?" Instead, we dive into whatever it is that would seem to fulfill our desires of the moment. By doing so, we often sacrifice what we want most for what we want now.

The classic "Marshmallow Study," conducted in the 1960s by Walter Michel with 5-year-old children, provided insight into the power of being able to delay gratification. The kids were challenged with either having one marshmallow at the moment or waiting 15 minutes and having two marshmallows. Those who could wait were found to do better over the next 20 years in terms of social relationships, academic performance and even emotional stability.

This doesn't mean we should always forgo what feels good or is desirable at the moment, but that we should consciously make decisions, focusing on what will lead to enduring happiness and not just instant gratification.

The "When/If" Dead End

Many of us put a "when" or "if" before our happiness. For instance: "I will be happy **when** I get my next promotion" or "I would be happy **if** my spouse treated me better." But by putting a "when" or an "if" in front of our happiness, we are putting our happiness off forever because there will always be another "when" and "if" to wait for. This tactic also puts our happiness into someone else's hands.

The stark reality is that no one and nothing is coming to make us happy. We create our own happiness. Titles, raises, accolades, money, vacations, houses, cars and other possessions will bring momentary feelings of happiness, but they do not sustain those feelings. Enduring happiness is an attitude that depends on no one else and nothing else.

I pursued this dead end for most of my life. At work I would think: "I will be happy when I get to be product manager;" then, "I will be happy when I am marketing manager;" then general manager; and on it went. In my personal life, I would think: "I'll be happy when we can own a home;" then, a bigger home; an even bigger home; a second home; or when I have so much saved; or when my golf handicap is single digit; or when I have a certain car. It was as if the distance between point "A" and point "B" was just an empty space or an obstacle to move through. What I have come to realize is that the distance between points "A" and "B" is life; it is where happiness is found. All of those little points were fine — with most being worthy of pursuit — but the achievement of them only brings momentary pleasure. It is the space in between that should be treasured. It's where the real happiness is found.

A couple of years ago, a Chinese student named Xinxin wrote me an email long after I had already closed out the class list. She wanted me to let her into the class even though it was full. The email was three pages long, but I wasn't convinced I should let her in until I got to the last line. Her email ended: "But Mr. Smith, whether you let me in the class or not, I will be happy." She knew her happiness was not dependent on me or on getting into the class, but on her. She was a wonderful addition to the class.

LIVING ON
THE OTHER SIDE
OF COMPLEXITY

Chapter 10

SIMPLICITY ON THE OTHER SIDE OF COMPLEXITY

*I have taken thousands of people across [the river],
and to all of them my river has been nothing but
a hindrance on their journey. They have traveled
for money and business, to weddings and on
pilgrimages; the river has been in their way and the
ferry man was there to take them quickly across the
obstacle. However, amongst the thousands there
have been a few, four or five, to whom the river
was not an obstacle. They have heard its voice and
listened to it and the river has become holy to them,
as it has to me.*

—Herman Hesse, *Siddhartha*

Maybe I am a slow learner. Certainly my father thought so
during my early years. As I struggled in elementary school,
I remember he kept the book *Why Johnny Can't Read*, by
Rudolf Franz Flesch, beside his bed. Since my older sisters
and brother were doing just fine in school, I am sure I was
the reason he was reading this book.

On the bright side, I was quick enough as a 7 year old to grasp this. I eventually did learn to read — and maybe even write. As a young adult, I discovered my own purposes in life and began to pursue them with passion and focus. My hope is that if he were living today, my father would no longer feel the need to study *Why Johnny Can't Read*.

But in some ways, I feel I am still a slow learner. Namely, because of the number of setbacks I have endured before grasping certain concepts and ideas, many of which are expressed in this book. The power of faith, optimism, forgiveness, strong relationships and abundance took me years to discover. I'm sure it would have been much more pleasant to reach this higher and deeper ground without the setbacks. But I am increasingly convinced many setbacks are unavoidable and that they have a very real and necessary purpose in our lives.

The challenges, losses, pain and sorrows of life spare no one. We will all encounter them. We must know pain to know pleasure, up to know down, loss to know gain, sorrow to know joy, darkness to know light. It sounds trite, but we can't have one without the other. Sorrow and joy are not opposites, but part of the complex web that makes up life.

An old Chinese proverb states, "The way to simplicity is through complexity." I think this is the same idea Oliver Wendell Holmes was offering, when he said, "I wouldn't give a fig for simplicity on this side of complexity, but I would give my life for simplicity on the other side of complexity."

"Complexity" is an interesting concept. I think in both statements, complexity refers to those times in our lives when things get jumbled up, confused, unhinged and discombobulated. It's when life throws us a curve ball and we end up with something unexpected, maybe undeserved and probably unwanted. The net effect is that we are challenged to give up old ways of thinking and forced to find new ways of coping.

Not every setback has led me to higher ground. Sometimes, I think I sank like a fence post in quicksand when challenged. I think we have four options when we encounter setbacks: We can become victims, we can survive, we can recover or we can thrive. Many times the outcome is up to us. We can choose between being victimized or thriving.

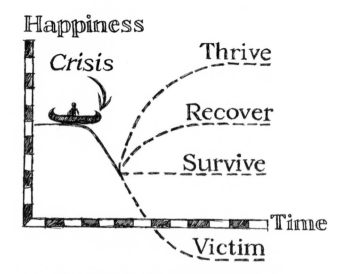

Modified from Sonja Lyubomirski, *The How of Happiness*

The question before us then is how best to deal with setbacks as we experience them. How do we make sure that we thrive and do not become victims? Here are six ideas to help us thrive in the face of crises:

1. **Know that this too shall pass.**

   When I face a setback, I have a tendency to think it will last forever. It won't, or at least the overwhelming feeling I have about the crisis won't. Nothing is forever. I try now to experience grief and sorrow while recognizing it as a stage, and only a stage, in the process of dealing with setbacks. I try to move through the stages of grief, reminding myself that no stage is permanent.

2. **Control the bleeding.**

   It helps to compartmentalize problems, as much as possible. Some folks are really good at enduring a crisis in one part of their life and not letting it dramatically affect the other parts. If they have a problem at home, they don't take it to work, and vice versa. Yes, it helps to share problems with others, but what I am suggesting is we don't let a crisis bleed into all aspects of our lives.

3. **Look for the purpose and meaning in crisis.**

   Setbacks don't necessarily happen for some preordained reason, but perhaps it is our task to find purpose or meaning in the things that happen to us. Often setbacks can be vehicles for new growth, new insights and the development of new strengths. Going through a setback successfully often boosts self-esteem and confidence. There is almost always something to learn from a setback, and it can be quite profound and life changing. As Garth Brooks sings in *The Dance*: "I could have missed the pain, but I'd have had to miss the dance."

4. Get help, give help.

When we are challenged, we are often tempted to keep it to ourselves and not reach out to others. But sharing a problem with a close friend or family member enables us to get clearer about what the challenge is, to gain insight from others and to enlist them in seeking solutions. It also just helps to simply know that others care.

At the same time, the best way to help ourselves may be just to help others. By helping others, we often set aside our own problems, realize how blessed we are, and discover new skills needed to solve our own challenges.

5. Connect with and care for self.

Get centered. We should take the time to understand who we are, what we care about, what we value so that we can make decisions that are consistent with who we are and who we want to be. Grief and sorrow are nature's way of having us slow down and replenish. Part of that replenishment is connecting to our souls and our spirituality.

6. Dig no holes (at least no deep holes).

Life will invariably hand us enough problems and setbacks that we don't need to create more for ourselves. If you are doing things that will bring you grief later, figure out how to stop doing them. If you smoke a pack of cigarettes a day, stop. If you drink to excess or use illegal drugs, stop. If you drink and drive, stop. If you are breaking major commitments you made to your spouse or significant other, stop. Figure out where you are digging holes that will be difficult to get out of in the future, and stop. Not digging holes can be very difficult, and to the degree you need to get assistance, do so. Dig no holes . . . at least no deep holes.

If you have read this far, you know that I like to use visual models to learn. This is probably another sign that I am a slow learner. A couple of years ago, I built a simple model around this concept of complexity and placed it on my mirror and my desk. On the left side I put things that I thought were on "this side" of complexity, and on the right side those things on the "other side" of complexity.

Here is the chart:

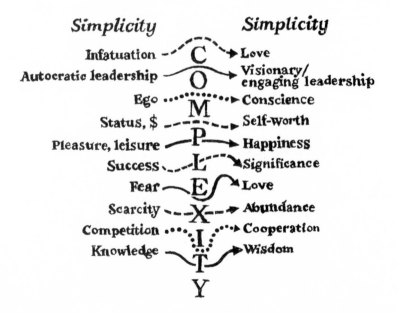

The "Other Side"

I wouldn't give a fig for simplicity on this side of complexity, but I would give my life for simplicity on the other side of complexity
— Oliver Wendell Holmes

Simplicity		*Simplicity*
Infatuation	C	Love
Autocratic leadership	O	Visionary/ engaging leadership
Ego	M	Conscience
Status, $	P	Self-worth
Pleasure, leisure		Happiness
Success	L	Significance
Fear	E	Love
Scarcity	X	Abundance
Competition	I	Cooperation
Knowledge	T	Wisdom
	Y	

Put simply, on the left side are concepts, ideas that at one point in my life I seemed to rely on. On the right side are concepts that I came to embrace and appreciate, and that have served me ever so much better. In most cases, I came to appreciate them only after going through the complexity of a setback. As I look at this chart, I realize that to the degree I can live on the right side of it, I am so much happier. There are probably hundreds of things you could put on this chart.

I think it is important also to realize that on the other side of complexity is not just simplicity, but another complexity, and beyond that, another complexity. Or as Christopher Fry states, "There will always be another reality to make fiction of the truth we think we have arrived at."

I will end this chapter with wisdom shared with me by two students in my class this past year. As we talked about setbacks and how to deal with them, one of the students, Willie, said jokingly, "I don't get setbacks." To which one of the other students, Carlos, said, "I don't get setbacks either; I get 'setforths.'"

What an incredible concept! Could we possibly come to consistently look at the setbacks we incur in life as being "setforths"? Yes, setbacks may often be painful. But can we search out and hold on to the greater wisdom, deeper values, new perspectives and new growth that come from the setbacks, so that on the other side of complexity, they become "setforths"? Such a perspective is worthy of our pursuit, since it will surely lead to greater happiness.

Sometimes the most unfortunate part of a setback is the failure to capitalize on the opportunity it presents for new growth, clearer insight, greater wisdom and a deeper appreciation for the life we have been given — the failure to turn "setbacks" into "setforths."

Chapter 11

THE FIVE THINGS

May God grant me grace, gratitude, courage, peace and time.

—Author, September 2, 2004

In the second chapter, I mentioned that on my long ride home from Rochester, Minnesota, to Columbus, Ohio, I asked for five things. By the end of that long night, I was no longer asking God to take the illness away, change the test results, or let the whole situation turn out to be just a bad dream. Rather, I asked for help finding and nurturing grace, gratitude, courage, peace and time.

Since my diagnosis, almost every day, I have asked for these five things. Ironically, however, while I have been asking for these, I have come to realize that it is, in fact, dealing with the illness that enables me to attain them. It is as if I am asking somebody for something they have already given me, but I just haven't recognized it. Let me explain.

The first thing I have been asking for is "grace." I'm not sure why I first asked for grace. In fact, I'm not even sure I knew what it meant, until I looked it up, then I understood why I wanted this trait. There are two definitions of grace that stood out to me: "unmerited divine assistance" and "the state of being pleasing to God." Now, nine years after my diagnosis, I do feel as if I have had undeserved divine intervention, and I deeply hope my life has been more pleasing to God.

The second thing I have been asking for is "gratitude." Since my diagnosis, I have come to appreciate that I am truly blessed. It may have taken major setbacks to realize it, but I live with the understanding that I have been blessed with far more than I could ever conceive of being worthy. My feeling of gratefulness for my life, my family and my work fills most every moment of my day. Gratitude has become the overarching sentiment in my life.

Even among those who consider themselves "cancer survivors," I have been blessed. I had 58 healthy years before being diagnosed. Since my diagnosis, I have felt fine the vast majority of the time. My treatments are not that difficult to handle and seem to have few side effects. My father learned he had cancer at what I now consider a fairly young age. He passed away within two months of the diagnosis. I have already lived nine years since my diagnosis.

I am blessed. My challenge will be to hold on to this feeling of gratitude, no matter what the illness has in store for me. To be able to deeply feel such gratitude — not just saying it, but feeling it — is an incredible blessing, brought to me by my illness. I also find that gratitude is a key source of my happiness.

"Courage" is the third thing I have asked for. In many ways, in our more difficult moments, the essence of all our virtues is courage, for without it, the other virtues mean little. I am embarrassed at times by my lack of courage; my unwillingness to stick by my principles when challenged; my allowing negative feelings to "snowball" and—right up there at the top—my fear of death.

This illness really does bring me face to face with my fear of death. I don't fear death as I once did. My desire to live is stronger than ever and I love my life. But death has lost its grip on me. My illness also tests my faith. If I want the trait of courage, confronting this illness and my own mortality offers the clearest pathway to develop and possess it.

Fourth, I have been asking for "peace." Released from the fear of death, there really is nothing else to fear. I am increasingly at peace. If, through this illness, I develop greater grace, gratitude and courage, it seems like peace will accompany them as well.

Finally, I have asked for "time." Now here is the really spooky part. At first glance, it would seem that this illness could not possibly give me time. After all, the doctors tell me it will rob me of time. So, if blood cancer actually shortens my life, how can it give me time?

Here is how. While time is finite and can be broken up into distinct measurable units — seconds, minutes, hours, days — like any resource, it can be squandered by one person and cherished and capitalized upon by another. With focus and understanding of one's purpose, with grace, gratitude, courage and peace, and with the help of family and friends, one year can be more fulfilling than 100 years in the hands of someone without these attributes. In other words, time can be a variable continuum.

Therefore, in a funny kind of way, this illness can give me time, no matter what the prognosis or the course that it takes.

Chapter 12

THE ONE THING

When all your desires are distilled you will cast just two votes: To love more and be happy.

—Hafiz

In the nine years since I was diagnosed with cancer, I have been on an incredible journey. I feel as if I am increasingly living on the "other side." At the same time, I recognize that on the other side of complexity lie more "other sides." With each challenge, we have the opportunity to travel further, to go deeper, to more fully grasp truth, to find deeper wisdom, to find simplicity on the other side of complexity.

My journey so far has also led me to the conclusion that at the foundation of happiness, at its core, is one thing: love. Without love, happiness is not possible. It is the love we have for ourselves and for others that leads to true joy. I am not alone in this belief.

George Vaillant has been the keeper of the Grant Study, the longest running longitudinal study in existence. The Grant study was formed between 1939 and 1944 and includes both Harvard students and inner-city youths. For the past 70-plus years, they have tracked almost every aspect of these people's lives. After studying how all of these participants have done, George Valliant made the following observation: "Relationships are the key to happiness. Happiness is love. Full Stop!"

In *Man's Search for Meaning*, referring to one morning while a prisoner in Auschwitz, Viktor Frankl writes:

> *We stumbled on in the darkness, over big stones and through large puddles, along the road leading from the camp. The accompanying guards kept shouting at us and driving us with the butts of their rifles. Anyone with very sore feet supported himself on his neighbor's arm. Hardly a word was spoken; icy wind did not encourage talk.*
>
> *Occasionally, I looked at the sky where the stars were fading and the pink light of morning was beginning to spread behind a dark bank of clouds. But my mind clung to my wife's image, imagining it with an uncanny acuteness. I heard her answering me, saw her smile, her frank and encouraging look. Real or not, her look was then more luminous than the sun, which was beginning to rise.*
>
> *A thought transfixed me: For the first time in my life I saw the truth as it is set into song by so many poets, proclaimed as the final wisdom by so many thinkers. The truth — that love is the ultimate and highest goal to which man can aspire. I grasped the meaning of the greatest secret that human poetry and human thought and belief have to impart. The salvation of man is through love and in love.*

Dan Baker in *What Happy People Know* states, "Love is the wellspring of happiness, renewable and everlasting."

Even Charles Darwin, the champion of "survival of the fittest," concluded, "Human goodness [love] may be stronger than any other instinct or motive."

Every person who studies the well-being of man comes to the same conclusion: Love is the key to successful living, love is the key to happiness.

The most fundamental decision we can make, regarding happiness, is to love: to care for ourselves, to care for others and to care for the world in which we live.

Love is the 14th skill of happiness. Love, like all of the skills of happiness, is a choice. May it be your choice.

Chapter 13

CALL ME MR. LUCKY

LOST DOG

Three-legged dog, has mange, missing right ear, broken tail, recently castrated . . . Answers to "Lucky."

—Restaurant poster in Hanover, N.H.

My journey to understand and better practice the skills of happiness has led me increasingly to live with joy. Oh, I have far to go before I practice the skills consistently, but I know I am making progress. I have also come to understand what a gift my life is. In fact, I have come to believe my life is beautiful.

I will describe a typical day in my life. Most mornings I wake up around 5:30–6:00 A.M. I throw back the covers from the bed and look at the big toe on my left foot. If I don't see a toe tag, I rejoice. I then look over at my wife and can't believe I am married to such a beautiful, loving, kind woman. My first words to her are usually, "Call me Mr. Lucky," to which she responds, "Call me Mrs. Lucky." I then jump—OK, I step; I am getting older—out of bed and begin the day.

When I look in the bathroom mirror, that nagging inner voice that used to scream at me a string of negative thoughts, barely whispers. It is still there, but it is a lot more timid than it used to be. When it does speak, I am able to recognize it for what it is: the voice of fear. I realize that I don't have to listen to it or respond to it. I think that nagging voice is also drowned out by the louder voice I hear expressing gratitude for the day that is about to begin.

LOST
THREE-LEGGED DOG

HAS MANGE,
MISSING RIGHT EAR,
BROKEN TAIL,
RECENTLY CASTRATED...
ANSWERS TO THE NAME
OF "LUCKY"

Most mornings I walk 3 to 4 miles. If I am alone, I wear my iPod and listen to music. As I walk, I look around thinking I am so blessed to be here. I say to myself, "Thank you for the trees, thank you for the grass, thank you for the sky, the clouds, the stars, the moon, the wind, the earth, my life, my wife, my sons, the ability to walk, to see, to hear, to speak, to think. . . ." I never run out of things to be thankful for.

If Gordon isn't "bagging" the customers at Kroger that day, he walks with me. I love my conversations with him. They are basic exchanges about simple, but meaningful things. We walk to a fitness center about 2 miles away, work out and then head to Starbucks, me for coffee and he for iced passion tea . . . unsweetened.

The people we encounter most mornings at Starbucks — Frank, a financial advisor; Guido, a retired professor and renowned mathematician; Tony, a policeman with the canine unit, with his dog, Amour, in tow; John, an author and executive coach; Kamal, a driver for a local hospital; Dave who works at the VA; and baristas Linda, Joyce, Chris, Stacey and Brenda — all move easily in and out of the conversation most mornings.

When I return home, I have breakfast with Phyllis and Gordon, and then I head off to the office. If I speak with Greg by phone during the day, my conversations with him are about more complex concepts and ideas than my conversations with Gordon. They are stimulating, but no more or less meaningful than those I have with Gordon. The conversations are different; both are cherished.

At the close of the day, I head home and have dinner with Phyllis and Gordon. Gordon heads off to bed around 9 p.m., and then Phyllis and I have time to ourselves for the next few hours. It too is cherished time. We share events from the day, read or watch something on TV. Then we head to bed. I reflect back on the day, give thanks for it, ask for forgiveness where I have come up short, place my head on the pillow and rest.

It's a pretty simple day, but I think my life is beautiful for two reasons. First, I am nothing more than a bunch of matter that happens to be blessed with the gift of life. Out of the billions and billions of objects in our universe, we seem to be the only planet that supports this unique thing we call life. I could far, far more likely have been some molten rock on some distant star that burned out 10 billion years ago. Instead I am a living, breathing, thinking creature of this world. What are the chances? We really are an impossibility, existing in an impossible world, in an impossible solar system, in an impossible universe. Why shouldn't I conclude that my life is beautiful?

The second reason my life is beautiful is more profound and inarguable. My life is beautiful because I decided it to be. It is a perspective, a way of seeing things, and that perspective is available to any of us. Our lives become beautiful because we decide they are beautiful. The second we decide our lives are beautiful, this decision ushers in a whole host of events and actions. We begin to treat our life like any other beautiful possession we have. If we think our lives are beautiful, we are far less likely to mess them up with drugs, anger, vengeance, excessive guilt or remorse, fear, hatred, jealousy, or any number of other destructive emotions and actions.

Your life and my life can be beautiful because we decide they are, and that decision is the fundamental decision of happiness.

EPILOGUE

As I write this in the closing months of 2013, I am nine years into my cancer. My original prognosis from the Mayo Clinic was that this illness would end my life somewhere between five and 10 years. That prognosis was probably not too far off, given the way my illness has progressed, except for two critical elements.

The first has been my response to a mono-clonal antibody by the name of "Rituxan." This drug has been used to treat many people with my illness. However, as my excellent oncologist, Dr. Tom Sweeney, likes to point out, I may hold the world record in terms of the number of times I have been infused with it and the years it has been effective. I have now received 48 infusions of Rituxan over an eight-year period. For many, the drug works for only one or two years.

Second, once Rituxan no longer works for me, there may well be another drug to extend my life. Ibrutinib is a kinase inhibitor that is in phase III trials at the James Cancer Center, where I am treated. Under the leadership of Dr. John Byrd, this new medicine is showing remarkable results in relapsed patients with CLL — and with relatively few side effects. The trial includes several patients that were in hospice care and are now living relatively normal lives. The expectation is that Ibrutinib will be approved in early 2014.

I am deeply indebted to Dr. Byrd and his team of researchers, my oncologist Dr. Sweeney, the work of the James Cancer

Center, the work of the Leukemia & Lymphoma Society, the many thousands of people involved in caring for those with cancer, and those dedicated to finding ways to manage and cure the illness of cancer. To all of you, I express my deep appreciation and gratitude. Without your help and care I would not be here, and with your help and care maybe, just maybe, I will be around another 10 or 20 years.

Thank you

APPENDIX

Skills That Lead to Happiness

Past
1. Forgiveness
2. Gratitude

Present
7. Doing now what I'm doing now
8. Honoring mind/ body/spirit
9. Being Altruistic
10. Thinking with abundance
11. Mastering our stories
12. Finding meaning/ purpose/flow
13. Cherishing relationships

Future
3. Faith
4. Optimism
5. Flexibility
6. Openness ("FOFO")

SKILLS SUMMARY

Within this book, I have covered in some detail skills that lead to happiness. My intent here is to summarize them for your future reference. They are skills that none of us will ever perfect, but becoming better at them will lead to greater happiness and, therefore, more successful living.

Skills that Lead to Peace with the Past

There are two key skills that lead to peace with the past. One removes negative events or hurts from our lives and the other magnifies the positive. That they increase happiness is simple arithmetic.

1. **Forgiveness**

   This is probably the most important skill of happiness and the most difficult to practice. By forgiving, we are eliminating negatives from our past. Forgiveness is actually two very distinct and separate skills: forgiving others and forgiving ourselves. Forgiving others is about releasing the desire for vengeance. Forgiving ourselves is about self-esteem and the belief that we are worthy of happiness, that we are worthy of moving on from mistakes we have made. There are four things we can do with hurts from the past: we can hold on to them, forget them, repress them, or forgive them. Forgiveness is the only action we can voluntarily take that leads to happiness. It is like Tide laundry detergent: "It gets the dirt out!" Some people suggest they have a right to be angry with someone. Of course they do, it wouldn't be forgiveness if they didn't have a right to be mad. But forgiveness, whether we are forgiving ourselves or someone else, is a gift we give ourselves. Therefore, it is we who suffer when we don't forgive.

2. **Gratitude**

Happiness is difficult without gratitude, and when we do feel grateful, it is hard not to be happy. Gratitude is a skill that enables us to focus on, appreciate and hold on to good things about our past. Researchers have found that if we simply write in a journal three things for which we are grateful at the end of each day, we measurably increase our level of happiness. Gratitude, like all the skills of happiness, is an attitude, a perspective. It is looking at the world around us and finding more to be thankful for than unhappy about.

Skills that Lead to Confidence in the Future

Much of the stress we face in life is caused by our fixed notion of how the future should unfold and our inability to adjust to the various diversions the future will invariably take. Planning for the future is great; being rigid about how it unfolds is not. We cannot control the future. Genuinely happy people face the future with four fundamental happiness skills I call **"FOFO,"** for Faith, Optimism, Flexibility and Openness.

3. **Faith**

Imagination without faith can be a very cruel master. Faith entails believing the universe is benevolent, and that while it may not bring us what we want, it will always bring us what we need.

4. **Optimism**

Happiness and optimism correlate almost one to one. We all have the ability to think both optimistically and pessimistically. Thinking optimistically is generally advantageous to our lives and our happiness. When we think optimistically, we deal more effectively with setbacks because we see them as temporary, specific to the event and controllable. This, in turn, encourages us to be more proactive. When we think pessimistically, we tend to see setbacks as permanent, pervasive and uncontrollable, and that leads to passivity.

5. **Flexibility**
In looking to the future we tend to see one pathway forward when, in fact, there are an infinite number of pathways. Being flexible enough to adjust to variations in life leads to greater happiness.

6. **Openness**
When the future doesn't turn out the way we expected, the happiest among us are open and accepting to new situations and new destinations, rather than being fixated on the future we originally perceived.

Skills that Lead to Finding Joy in the Present

Happiness is found in the present and within ourselves. The happiest among us have a set of skills that enables them to live in and relish the present and look deeply within themselves and find happiness.

7. **Doing now what I am doing now**
Happiness is found in the present, but you must be present to find it. Most of us can read the paper, watch TV and carry on a conversation all at once. The problem is we do none of these activities well. Multitasking leads to stress and unhappiness.

8. **Honoring mind/body/spirit**
Taking care of ourselves leads to greater self-esteem and happiness. One of the keys to doing this is to continually

ask ourselves to whom and to what do we give access to our minds, our bodies and our spirits, and then to give access to those things and people that lead to lasting joy, rather than momentary pleasure.

9. **Being altruistic**
Overcoming the fear of "I won't have enough" and using our talents, passions, time and resources for the benefit of others actually lights up the pleasure centers of our brains.

10. **Thinking with abundance**
Comparison is the thief of joy. Those who are happiest among us realize it is an abundant world and focus more on cooperation than competition.

11. **Mastering our stories**
Most of us have an internal voice that is speaking (often shouting) at us during every waking moment. We are better than that internal voice. Becoming a master of, rather than a slave to, our internal voice is a key to happiness.

12. **Finding purpose/meaning**
Man is a searcher of meaning. Using our talents and devoting our energies to things we deem of value leads to happiness. When we find the intersection of what we love doing, what we are skilled at and what the world needs, our efforts will bring us intense joy.

13. **Cherishing relationships**
Those who live with joy create and nurture healthy relationships and do not trade off those relationships for purpose.

~

There is a fourteenth skill that underlies the other thirteen. In life we are either driven by fear or we are inspired by love. While we may meet with "success," as defined by our society, through fear, fear makes it difficult to live joyfully. We invariably pay a price when we are driven by fear. The fourteenth skill is love. It is the practice of caring for self, caring for others and caring for the world around us. Happiness is fundamentally a love of life and a life of love.

May your journey be one of love.

MORE ABOUT THE AUTHOR

Doug Smith is a successful business executive, who has served as chief executive of Kraft Foods Canada, chairman and CEO of Borden Foods Corporation, and chairman and CEO of Best Brands Corporation. Since 2004, he has dedicated himself to learning about, practicing and sharing that which enables people to live and lead abundantly. For the past seven years, he has taught the most popular winter term course at DePauw University: The Skills of Happiness.

He frequently lectures at Canyon Ranch in Lenox, Massachusetts, and Tucson, Arizona. He is a sought after speaker for corporate and educational events and conferences. Doug does this without compensation, but requires a meaningful donation to cancer research in return for his work.

Happiness, The Art of Living with Peace, Confidence and Joy is his first book. All of his profits from the book are donated directly to cancer research. Doug has an MBA from Dartmouth College and a BA and honorary doctorate from DePauw University. He and his wife Phyllis have two grown sons and live happily in Columbus, Ohio.

Should you wish to know more about Doug and his work, or contact him, you can find him at whitepinemountain.com.

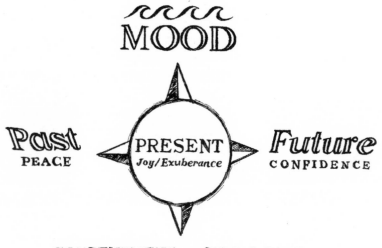